There Is No

Right Way To Do

A Wrong Thing

"So Vince Lombardi was wrong. Winning is not the only thing as headlines and hearings from Wall Street to Washington confirm. Now comes a better game plan from the powerful one-two punch of Ken Blanchard and Norman Vincent Peale in a quick-reading new book, *The Power of Ethical Mangement*. Peale and Blanchard may be the best thing that has happened to business ethics since Mike Wallace invented *60 Minutes*."

> —JOHN MACK CARTER
> Editor-in-Chief
> *Good Housekeeping*

"*The Saturday Evening Post* recommends this eloquent book to all who want to be successful managers in business. The book states beautifully what we at the *Post* have long believed, that by and large, men and women of integrity succeed in business far more frequently than those who operate without ethics."

> —CORY SERVASS, M.D.
> Editor and President
> *The Saturday Evening Post*

"There are very few shortcuts worth taking in life. Those people that truly succeed usually make it happen through hard work and honest relationships. Thank you to Drs. Blanchard and Peale for reinforcing that very important message."

> —PETE NEWELL
> 1960 Olympic Basketball Coach and
> Basketball Hall of Famer

"Praise the Lord. Two courageous men have brought back the words *integrity* and *ethical* into our business world. In my opinion, this book should be required reading for all MBA students."

> —BONITA GRANVILLE WRATHER
> Chairman of the Board
> Wrather Corporation

"With *The Power of Ethical Management*, my good friend Norman Vincent Peale and his new partner, Kenneth Blanchard, add a whole new wing on to the mansion of American self-help literature. There are many lessons packed into this parable for moderns."

> —W. CLEMENT STONE
> Founder of *Success Magazine*

The Power of Ethical Management

The One Minute Manager
Keith Blanchard and Spencer Johnson, 1982

Other books co-authored by Kenneth Blanchard

The Family Game: A Situational Approach to Effective Parenting
Leadership and the One Minute Manager
Management of Organizational Behavior:
Utilizing Human Resources
The One Minute Manager Gets Fit
Organizational Change Through Effective Leadership
Putting the One Minute Manager to Work

The Power of Positive Thinking
Norman Vincent Peale, 1952

Other books by Norman Vincent Peale

The Amazing Results of Positive Thinking
The Art of Real Happiness
Enthusiasm Makes the Difference
Faith is the Answer
A Guide to Confident Living
The Positive Principle Today
Stay Alive All Your Life
The Tough-Minded Optimist
The Joy of Positive Living
You Can If You Think You Can
Power of the Plus Factor
Inspiring Messages for Daily Living
The New Art of Living
Positive Thoughts for the Day
The Positive Way to Change Your Life
Power of Positive Thinking for Young People
Unlock Your Faith Power

The Power of Ethical Management

Kenneth Blanchard

Norman Vincent Peale

CEDAR

An imprint of William Heinemann Limited

Published by Cedar Books
an imprint of William Heinemann Limited
Michelin House, 81 Fulham Road, London SW3 6RB
LONDON   MELBOURNE   AUCKLAND

Copyright © 1988 by Blanchard Family Partnership and
Dr. Norman Vincent Peale

First published by William Morrow and Company Inc,
105 Madison Avenue, New York, NY 10016, USA

First published in Great Britain by Heinemann Kingswood, 1988
First published as a Cedar book 1990

0 434 11162 7

Printed in Great Britain
by Cox and Wyman Limited, Reading, Berks.

To
our wives,
Marjorie McKee Blanchard
and
Ruth Stafford Peale,
for
the strength of
their companionship
and
the influence
of their thinking
on
our lives

Introduction

In writing a book on ethics we are reminded of the story of a young Englishman who had just been elected to Parliament. When he entered the halls for the first time, he approached one of the sages and asked, "Tell me, sir, do you think I should participate in the debate today?"

The old man looked at him with piercing eyes and said, "To be honest, young man, I would recommend that you keep silent. It's better that people wonder why you didn't speak than wonder why you did."

The same advice might apply to the authors of a book on ethics in business. We know we are taking a risk by speaking out on such a sensitive topic, but we feel it is important to do so.

Everywhere we turn today there are signs of ethical deterioration. In business, bright young people have made immoral millions by using insider trading information. In government, hardly a day goes by without some public official being involved in an ethical dilemma on Capitol Hill. In education, cheating scandals among students and under-the-table payments to college athletes by alumni have become commonplace.

Obviously, all these people, many of them supposedly outstanding citizens, believed that they had to cheat to win. They, along with many others, believe that nice guys finish last. We, however, disagree.

Shortly after we were introduced to each other by Larry Hughes, president of the Hearst Trade Book Group and former president of William Morrow and Company, we discovered that we believed in many of the same things.

Both of us agree that ethical behavior is related to self-esteem. We both believe that people who feel good about themselves have what it takes to withstand outside pressure and to do what is right rather than do what is merely expedient, popular, or lucrative. We believe that a strong code of morality in any business is the first step toward its success. We believe that ethical managers are winning managers.

This book hopes to prove these points.

Dealing with such a topic as ethics is like untangling a fishing line. The more you get into it, the more complicated it becomes. In fact, a number of people have told us, "You're brave men to speak out on ethics." However, being positive thinkers, we weren't easily dissuaded by such warnings. Throughout our careers we both tried to take seemingly complicated issues and talk about them in simple language that can be easily understood. That's what *The One Minute Manager* and *The Power of Positive Thinking* both did.

This book is written in a parable format because both of us believe that stories are the best way to teach. We invite you to be the troubled manager in this story. In doing this, try to resist any urge you may have to discount the applicability of the circumstances of this story because they do not exactly correspond to your own situation or environment. Even though you may not be a sales manager—or you may not even work in business—the type of situation that we have portrayed reflects common elements of any ethical dilemma. As a result, there is learning for all of us in this single scenario.

We hope the following pages will give you the knowledge to better sort the dilemmas you face and the inspiration to act in a way that is ethically consistent with your beliefs. We hope that what we say here will help make your life, and the lives of the people you care about and work with, even brighter, more productive, and happier.

The Power of Ethical Management is for everyone who faces ethical dilemmas in their lives. It is also for managers who want to know what they can do to help create a healthy work environment where people don't have to cheat to win.

—KENNETH BLANCHARD
NORMAN VINCENT PEALE
1988

Contents

I WAS sitting at home in my favorite easy chair, but my mind was not at rest. It was 4:00 a.m. For the third night in a row I'd awakened in the early hours, troubled and confused by a problem at work that increasingly gnawed at me.

Being a division sales manager for a large high-tech company in a very competitive industry can have its difficult moments. This definitely was one of them. Sales had been down for almost six months and my boss was putting pressure on me to get my division's numbers up. I'd been involved for a month in a search for a topflight, experienced sales representative to add to my sales force, and three days ago I had interviewed a very likely prospect.

From the moment he walked confidently into my office, I'd felt this man was just the person I needed. As the interview proceeded I became more and more excited. It was obvious that I'd be lucky to get this person. He had an outstanding sales record and knew our industry backward and forward. Most intriguingly, he had just quit a top job with our major competitor, after six successful years with that company.

Throughout our meeting, I realized that this sales representative was head and shoulders above all other applicants I had interviewed, in every category. I'd just about made up my mind to hire him (pending a phone call or two to check his references), when he smiled, reached into his attaché case, and pulled out a small, square envelope. From it he extracted a computer disc, and held it up as if it were a priceless gem.

"Can you guess what's on this disc?" he said.

I shook my head.

Still smiling, his voice oozing with self-assurance, he proceeded to explain that the disc contained a wealth of confidential information about our competitor, his former employer—including profiles of all their customers and cost data on a major defense-contract bid for which our company was also competing. As we closed out the interview session, he promised me that, if I hired him, he would give me this disc and more of the same.

After he left my office, I had two immediate responses to what had just happened. The first reaction was one of rage. How could he *do* such a thing? I knew that what he proposed was wrong and because of that he wasn't the kind of person I wanted on my team. My second reaction was not as quick or as emotional, but when it surfaced I knew it was something I could not easily dismiss. The more I thought about it, the more I realized that this person was offering me and our company a virtual gold mine. He had told me enough to convince me that if I hired him, I could, most likely, bring in not only the giant defense contract but several other huge accounts—fish I'd been angling for over the past three years. It was all there within my grasp. I knew it was one of those once-in-a-lifetime opportunities. And I certainly could use such an opportunity now.

With one of our kids already in college and two more close behind, my wife and I were starting to feel a financial pinch. Without a promotion of some kind, I felt things were going to get worse before they got better. There was no better opportunity than now for a promotion because the executive vice-president in charge of sales and marketing was retiring and my boss would be moving up. His replacement was the subject of the loudest hush-hush there had been in our company since I'd been there. With the current sagging sales record of my division, I had thought I didn't have a chance. But that was before my interview with this sales representative. This would be the perfect time for me to land a large new contract.

I realized that I was caught somewhere between the two reactions of rage and temptation and I decided to go to talk to one of our senior operations managers about the situation. He had been a mentor to me ever since I'd joined the company twelve years before. After I had told him the whole story, his reply was short and to the point, and it surprised me. What he said was "Hire this guy before someone else does. I know it's a risk, but everyone in our industry tries to get reliable data on competitors any way they can. We stand to lose a real *competitive edge* if you don't strike while the iron's hot." The way he said "competitive edge" was, I knew, a mimic of my boss, who was always hitting us with those words and in that tone.

As I left his office, he patted my shoulder and winked as he assured me he knew I'd do the sensible thing.

As I wandered down the hall toward my office, I ran into my top assistant, a sharp, aggressive M.B.A. graduate. She said, "You look troubled. Anything wrong?"

I quickly motioned her to follow me to my office. Once inside I shut the door and spilled out the whole story, again. Her response was the exact opposite of my mentor's. She looked me straight in the eye and said, "Listen. Think about what you're contemplating here. Not only is what this guy doing wrong, but if you hire him, you would be supporting that kind of behavior. Besides, there's no telling when he might start stealing from *us* and selling to the highest bidder." I nodded; I'd thought of this myself. "And," she went on, "if the story ever gets out that you hired him knowing he had stolen confidential information, the whole thing could blow up in your face and give our company a bad name."

After she'd left, I sat there realizing that my two associates, rather than helping me, had made my decision more difficult. I wondered what I should do. Hire him or say "Thanks, but no thanks." Or maybe hire him but tell him not to bring stolen information. "But could I trust him to be honest once he started to work here?" I wondered. "Then again, maybe I should just turn him in—call his former boss."

These questions had kept me awake in the middle of the night as I played mental gymnastics with the issues. I knew in my heart that what he was doing was wrong. And I also knew that it sometimes takes guts to stand up for what one knows is right. But at the same time, I didn't want to be naïve. If others were doing this kind of thing—and competitors would jump at a chance to get reliable information and sales talent all wrapped up in one package—maybe I *should* hire him.

I didn't know where else to turn for advice. My boss was at corporate headquarters in Chicago and everything that came out of his mouth or through the mail had to do with improving the bottom line. The vice-president of our division was retiring and seemed to have mentally dropped out of company affairs. The president was an unknown quantity to me—I rarely saw him and knew nothing about his views on business ethics.

I realized I needed to ask the advice of someone who was not directly involved in the situation. Three sleepless nights in a row was enough. I hadn't decided to hire this salesperson, but I also hadn't decided not to hire him. "How's that for a double negative?" I thought, smiling for the first time in days.

AN OLD college friend came to mind. We had been student-government leaders together and had kept in contact over the years. Last year her company had been involved in a widespread scandal because some executives had falsified time sheets and overcharged the government. Since then a new president had been brought in. He had quickly appointed an ethical ombudsman to hear complaints of wrongdoing, created a new Code of Ethics and Standards of Conduct policy, had the company's time cards stamped with an explicit warning that mischarging was a crime, and installed a mandatory ethics training program for personnel at all levels of the organization. As part of this new regime my friend had been given a two-year appointment as the company's ethics officer to help with the new ethics program and related training. Knowing her as I did, I was not surprised by this appointment. Her integrity and sense of fair play had always been beyond reproach.

I WAS lucky that she agreed to meet with me that evening. Throughout my tale she listened thoughtfully. When I finished my story, I asked, "If someone in your company were to come to you with such a dilemma, what would you suggest?"

"I'd give that person the *Ethics Check*," she said.

"The Ethics Check?"

"Yes. The Ethics Check helps individuals to sort out dilemmas by showing them how to examine the problem at several different levels. It has three questions, each of which clarifies a different aspect of the decision. The Ethics Check helps to take the grayness out of ethical situations.

"It seems," she continued, "that there are a lot of people in our country today who have put themselves into stressful situations because they have knowingly made unethical decisions—decisions that they basically know are morally wrong. In our company that certainly was true. Many people contend that nowadays there is a big gray area between right and wrong, and they use that gray area as an excuse not to worry about being ethical. We question that logic. We've come to the realization that a lot of the grayness can be taken out of ethical dilemmas if one takes the time to sort out the situation. It is easy to charge ahead without thinking and then rationalize your behavior after the fact. But the fact of the matter is:

*

There
Is
No
Right
Way
To
Do
A
Wrong
Thing

*

My FRIEND continued, "We feel that most people basically know right from wrong, but it helps clarify issues if they can answer three questions when confronted with an ethical problem."

I got out my note pad.

"The first question is straightforward: *Is it legal?*"

I wrote that down. Then I looked up to find my friend's eyes fixed on me questioningly. "Well," she said, "is it?"

"I have no trouble answering that one," I said. "My answer has to be a resounding 'no' when it comes to this sales representative. He is stealing proprietary information."

My friend nodded. "Our company feels that if you give a 'no' answer to that first question, then you don't even have to consider the next two questions." She paused a moment, looking thoughtful. "However, I'm not sure I completely agree. So I always tell people they should answer all the questions before making any final judgment."

"When you say 'legal,' are you talking only about civil or criminal law?"

"No," said my friend. "We also take into consideration company policy. In our case, that now includes our new Code of Ethics and Standard of Conduct policy."

"What's that policy about?"

"It states that each of our employees is responsible for both the integrity and the consequences of his or her own actions. The highest standards of honesty, integrity, and fairness must be followed by each and every employee when engaging in any activity concerning the company, particularly in relationships with customers, competitors, suppliers, the public, and other employees.

"The big picture, though," she continued, "is that our company now expects that no employee will undertake any activity while on company premises, or while engaging in company business, that is (or gives the appearance of being) improper, illegal, or immoral, or that could in any way harm or embarrass our company or our customers."

Marveling at her ability to state her company's policy on ethical expectations with such clarity, I said, "Our company certainly could use a policy like that."

"It's a clear message from the top about what kind of company we want to be," said my friend. "But before you praise us, remember—this new policy is part of a response to unethical behavior that was discovered to be previously widespread throughout our company."

"**W**ELL, it certainly is a good start to turning things around," I said. "It also makes me realize that a company needs to have a clear and written policy if it is to expect and encourage ethical behavior from its employees. What's the second question in the Ethics Check?"

"Is it balanced?" said my friend. "By that we mean, is the decision going to be fair or will it heavily favor one party over another in the short or the long term."

"You mean," I said, writing down the second question, "is there clearly going to be a big winner or a big loser? It makes me think of the rash of unfriendly takeovers that have recently been occurring, in which short-term stockholders and deal-makers make a killing while many employees often lose."

"That's a good example," she nodded. "Our feeling is that lopsided, win-lose decisions invariably end up as lose-lose situations. In other words, if any individual in our company makes a decision that benefits that person or our company at someone else's real expense—be it another employer, a supplier, a customer, or even a competitor—it will eventually come back to haunt the individual or the company. Everyone cannot win equally on every situation all the time, but we want to avoid major imbalances over the course of our relationships."

I thought of my own case and said, "If I decide to hire this sales representative and use his inside information, that would clearly be a big win for our company and a big loss for our competitor."

"Right," said my friend. "And when it becomes clear what has happened, your competitor will look for ways to get even. They'll be asking themselves what top people they can pirate from you or what information they can get on your company to use against you."

"Our relationship could end up far worse than just being competitive in the marketplace," I suggested.

"And while you are playing one-upmanship with each other," she said, "another competitor may very well pass you both by. Or even worse, you may both give your industry a bad name. The more the managers in our company have talked about ethics, the more we realized that our company loyalty ought also to be to our industry. There's no peace of mind in being Number One in a troubled industry. If customers begin to mistrust people in your company, everyone's business is affected."

"I wish I could trust that our competitor wouldn't hire one of our people in a similar situation," I said. "But when I ask myself if it's fair for me to hire this sales representative—with his confidential information—the answer is clearly 'No!' Even though I already have two nos, what's the last question on this Ethics Check?"

"**T**HE last is the clincher," said my friend. "Everyone contemplating an ethical decision should ask himself or herself: *How will it make me feel about myself?*"

"I'm surprised that's a question. I thought that by asking whether it was legal, you were advocating *right* regardless of how it makes you feel."

"That's why we chose three questions. The legal question gets you to look at existing standards; the balance question activates your sense of fairness and rationality; and this last question focuses on your emotions and your own standards of morality."

"So you're suggesting that if you do something that goes against your own innate sense of what's right, you can't help but feel bad," I stated.

"Yes," she answered. "An unethical act will erode self-esteem. Questions like 'How would I feel if what I'm considering doing was published in the newspaper?' Or 'Would I like my family to know?' also get at this issue. When it comes to what enhances and what detracts from your own feelings of self-esteem, John Wooden, the legendary UCLA basketball coach, said it well:

*

There
Is
No Pillow
As
Soft
As A
Clear
Conscience

*

"That certainly hits home with me," I said. "Ever since I was confronted with this ethical issue, I haven't been able to sleep."

"All your restlessness probably means that your conscience is wrestling with your survival instincts. You're trying to reach your career objectives and still do what is right. You see," she continued, "I think your conscience was telling you from the very beginning that what the salesman intended to do was wrong. He was stealing—and if you hired him, you would be condoning this unethical behavior, wouldn't you?"

"I sure would!"

"What has had your conscience working overtime and has kept you awake is the realization that you were seriously considering doing something you knew was wrong because it might help your career in the short run. Isn't that the issue?"

"That's definitely it," I agreed. "And that hasn't made me feel very pleased with myself. This Ethics Check of yours is very helpful. I can see how it can help someone to decide what is right." With that, I took a moment to jot down some notes, while my friend waited. Then I said, "Let me make sure I have the three questions right."

THE "ETHICS CHECK" QUESTIONS

1. *Is it legal?*
   Will I be violating either civil law or
   company policy?

2. *Is it balanced?*
   Is it fair to all concerned in the short term
   as well as the long term? Does it promote
   win-win relationships?

3. *How will it make me feel about myself?*
   Will it make me proud?
   Would I feel good if my decision was
   published in the newspaper?
   Would I feel good if my family knew about
   it?

G LANCING at my notes, my friend said, "Those responsible for ethics training find that constant use of the Ethics Check questions can guide all of us into a pattern of 'right' behavior that will become habit-forming.

"Many managers just need a little guidance and support to make the right choice," my friend continued. "Now that you have sorted things out for yourself, maybe you can set an example for others. At our company, we try to make our managers understand that they not only have an obligation to the company to do what is right but also have an obligation to those people who report to them and look to them for leadership. You could have a significant influence on the people around you."

"So you think guidance from the top is needed to bring out the best in people?" I asked.

"Most definitely," answered my friend. "I can't say enough about the importance of setting an example. For instance, so many parents look the other way when they see their kids do something wrong. I'm sure this is also true of managers in business. The usual excuse is 'Everybody does it or allows it—why should I take a stand?'"

"That's certainly like some of the advice I've been getting on hiring this dishonest sales representative," I said.

"And yet when you avoid confronting an ethical issue," she continued, "you essentially are saying it's OK. And if you do that, you are setting a bad example. I'll never forget an article published in the *Chicago Sun Times,* by Jack Griffin, called 'It's OK, Son, Everybody Does it.'" She reached into her handbag. "I brought along a copy."

IT'S OK, SON, EVERYBODY DOES IT

BY

JACK GRIFFIN

When Johnny was 6 years old, he was with his father when they were caught speeding. His father handed the officer a twenty dollar bill with his driver's license. "It's OK, son," his father said as they drove off. "Everybody does it."

When he was 8, he was present at a family council presided over by Uncle George, on the surest means to shave points off the income tax return. "It's OK, kid," his uncle said. "Everybody does it."

When he was 9, his mother took him to his first theater production. The box office man couldn't find any seats until his mother discovered an extra $5 in her purse. "It's OK, son," she said. "Everybody does it."

When he was 12, he broke his glasses on the way to school. His Aunt Francine persuaded the insurance company that they had been stolen and they collected $75. "It's OK, kid," she said. "Everybody does it."

When he was 15, he made right guard on the high school football team. His coach showed him how to block and at the same time grab the opposing end by the shirt so the official couldn't see it. "It's OK, kid," the coach said. "Everybody does it."

When he was 16, he took his first summer job at the supermarket. His assignment was to put the overripe strawberries in the bottom of the boxes and the good ones on top where they would show. "It's OK, kid," the manager said. Everybody does it."

When he was 18, Johnny and a neighbor applied for a college scholarship. Johnny was a marginal student. His neighbor was in the upper 3 percent of his class, but he couldn't play right guard. Johnny got the scholarship. "It's OK, son," his parents said. "Everybody does it."

When he was 19, he was approached by an upperclassman who offered the test answers for $50. "It's OK, kid," he said, "Everybody does it."

Johnny was caught and sent home in disgrace. "How could you do this to your mother and me?" his father said. "You never learned anything like this at home." His aunt and uncle were also shocked.

If there's one thing the adult world can't stand, it's a kid who cheats. . . .

Updated from the
Chicago Sun Times

"This article hits the nail on the head," I said. "No wonder that boy cheated. No one ever set a good example for him."

"Even inaction may send a bad message," she said, "because someone may be watching to see if you tell a clerk when he has given you too much change or stop for a red light even when there is no one around."

"Thanks for helping me sort things out and making me aware of the importance of setting an example," I said as I shook my friend's hand and told her again how much I appreciated her time.

"We lose our focus from time to time," she concluded with a smile. "We can make all kinds of excuses to ourselves to justify our own unethical actions but ultimately we harm ourselves. This Ethics Check can help keep things in focus."

AS I headed home, I felt better about myself. I knew I was going to have my first good night's sleep in three days.

When my wife saw my face, she smiled. "I can tell you've made a good decision."

That evening I reviewed the situation. Until then I had considered hiring the questionable sales rep, but telling him not to bring any stolen information with him. But now I realized fully that I really didn't want a person on my team I couldn't trust. I didn't need the aggravation of worrying about whether this man would be stealing my company's secrets. I decided to keep looking for a qualified sales representative.

But did my commitment to behave ethically end with my decision not to hire the salesman? Should I report him to his former employer? That question crossed my mind several times. While the possibility was slight that I could be considered an accomplice if I didn't report his actions, I wasn't ready to take on the responsibility of possibly ruining this guy's career. That wouldn't make me feel very good about myself either. So, instead, I decided to be straight with the man and tell him exactly why I wasn't hiring him.

The next morning the first person I called when I got to work was my mentor. I told him I had decided to pass on the sales representative. "While I know he was well qualified and it would have been helpful to have his inside information, in the long run I think I would have had trouble living with myself. What he was doing was illegal and a decision to hire him would have been grossly unfair to our competition."

"I respect your decision," my mentor said, "but I think you're naïve. This is a tough, competitive industry. Sure there was a risk that he might do the same to us, but I think the Golden Rule of Business applies here: 'Do unto others what they would do unto you if the roles were reversed.' Our competitors would have hired that guy in a minute. Don't brag about your decision to your boss. I don't think he'd be sympathetic."

I was disappointed, but his response was not completely unexpected.

My top aide's reaction was more gratifying. "You made the right decision," she said. "Remember the old adage: 'What goes around comes around.' If you had hired that sales representative with his stolen information, the decision eventually would have come back to haunt you and possibly the company as well."

I THEN called the sales rep and I told him that even though he was the most qualified candidate for the position, I wasn't going to hire him. Then I told him why. When I finished speaking, he said, "You've just passed up the best chance you'll have in years to gain on your competition."

I decided to tell all my salespeople what had happened and to talk with them about establishing a code of ethics for our department. When I met with them later in the week, I said, *"If we have to cheat to win, then we'd better think twice about what we're doing."* As I discussed the sales-representative incident and my beliefs about ethical behavior, I could see by their faces I was getting mixed reviews. In fact, one of my top salespeople said, "What about last week's memo from the home office? It's pretty clear that we had better do something about our numbers—and fast—or there could be some shakeups in our department."

I knew well what he was talking about. The pressure was on now more than ever before. That memo from my boss had a threatening tone. To me, and to other managers at my level, the message was loud and clear: "I don't care how you get the results—just get them." This highlighted for me one of the knottiest problems facing business: *How can you get acceptable bottom-line results, stay competitive, and at the same time, be committed to ethical practices?*

To me, this question raised another and more personal question: *How do you act on your good intentions?* The Ethics Check questions were helpful in sorting out what the right decision should be, but they didn't provide any guidelines about how to go about doing what was right.

When I got home that night I talked to my wife about the pressures I was feeling. I told her I believed the most difficult aspect of being ethical was *doing* what was right, not *deciding* what was right. "Driving home tonight," I said, "I realized that I don't have any strategy for acting ethically when I'm confronted by pressures that run counter to what I know is right. I could use some advice about implementing ethical decisions."

My wife remembered a close friend of her parents, someone who had been an inspiration to them. He was a minister and, more recently, a motivational speaker, who advised people from all walks of life. "Why don't you call him?" she urged. "I'm sure he would be interested in your situation. He's a real positive thinker."

I called the advisor and made an appointment to see him the following week.

WHEN I arrived at his office, I was greeted by a man with a friendly face and a warm handshake. The advisor was as vibrant and enthusiastic as my wife had described. Everything about him and his office made me feel at home.

As we sat down, I began to tell him about the ethical dilemma I had been facing lately. I told him all about the sales representative, the lack of support for ethical behavior in my organization, and the conversation I had had with my friend about the Ethics Check questions.

"It's clear that you have a real challenge with this issue. When I have been faced with similar dilemmas in the past," he said thoughtfully, "I try to remember that we are given the freedom to choose to live ethically or choose to live otherwise. Having this freedom to choose, and exercising it with integrity and humility, actually makes us strong. It's analogous to building up physical strength. Every time you work out, you deal with resistance. If the weights are too light to provide that resistance—and therefore easy for you to lift—you won't increase your strength. That's why the toughest ethical problems provide the biggest opportunities for growth.

"**I**F YOU are always confronted with easy choices, you don't build *character*," continued the advisor. "Free will puts us into situations like the one you have described, and working on them stretches us."

"You certainly live up to your reputation," I smiled. "My wife said you were a positive thinker."

"Well, *I am* a positive thinker," said the advisor, "because positive thinkers get positive results. Inevitably! Indubitably!"

Laughing, I said, "Now I don't know exactly what that last word means, but I like the sound of it. Why do positive thinkers get positive results?"

"One reason is that they're not afraid of what we call a 'problem.' Now I know that the minute you mention the word 'problem' the inference is that you are talking about something that is a negative and ought to be gotten rid of as fast as possible. But nothing could be further from the truth."

"You don't think life would be better if we had fewer problems?"

"I'll answer that question by telling you a story," said the advisor. "One day I was walking down the street, when I saw my friend George approaching. It was evident from his downtrodden look that he wasn't overflowing with the ecstasy and exuberance of human existence, which is a high-class way of saying George was dragging bottom.

"Naturally I asked him, 'How are you, George?' While that was meant to be a routine inquiry, George took me very seriously and for fifteen minutes he enlightened me on how bad he felt. And the more he talked the worse *I* felt.

"Finally I said to him, 'Well, George, I'm sorry to see you in such a depressed state. How did you get this way?' That really set him off.

"'It's my problems,' he said. 'Problems— nothing but problems. I'm fed up with problems. If you could get me rid of all my problems, I would contribute $5,000 to your favorite charity.'

"Well now, I am never one to turn a deaf ear to such an offer, and so I meditated, ruminated, and cogitated on the proposition and came up with an answer that I thought was pretty good.

"I said, 'Yesterday I went to a place where thousands of people reside. As far as I could determine, not one of them has any problems. Would you like to go there?'

"'When can we leave? That sounds like my kind of place,' answered George.

"'If that's the case, George,' I said, 'I'll be happy to take you tomorrow to Woodlawn Cemetery because the only people I know who don't have any problems are dead.'"

I let out a laugh. "I guess having problems is a fact of life," I concluded.

"Indeed," said my advisor. "It's even possible that the more problems you have, the more alive you may be. And if you have no problems at all—I warn you—you're in grave jeopardy—you're on the way out and you don't know it! In fact, if you really don't believe you have any problems, I suggest that you immediately race from my office, jump into your car, drive home, run into your house, and go straight to your bedroom and slam the door. Then get down on your knees and pray:

*

*What's
The
Matter,
Lord?
Don't
You
Trust
Me
Anymore?
Give
Me
Some
Problems!*

*

"**T**HE Lord trusts me all right," I laughed. "I have plenty of problems. Just sorting out these ethical issues has kept me very busy."

"A person of principle has to be clearheaded and decisive in order to act in a manner consistent with his or her values," said the advisor.

"You hit upon the main issue for me," I said. "How do you behave ethically when there are so many pressures not to do so? You mentioned the analogy of lifting with enough weight to build up strength. How do you build up inner strength so you can resist external pressure and consistently do what you know is right in a difficult situation?"

"What you have to learn are the five core principles of ethical decision-making. I call them the *Five P's of Ethical Power*."

"The Five P's of Ethical Power?" I echoed. Once again, I took out my trusty note pad.

"The five core principles of ethical behavior are also the ingredients for genuine, lasting fulfillment in life. Highly successful, satisfied individuals practice these Five P's with great consistency."

"What are they?" I eagerly asked.

"For now," continued the advisor, "let me write all five down on your note pad." I handed him my pencil and he wrote:

*

The Five P's Of Ethical Power

Purpose
•
Pride
•
Patience
•
Persistence
•
Perspective

*

"As you can see, the first principle of ethical power is *Purpose*," said my advisor. "By purpose, I mean your objective or intention— something toward which you are always striving."

"Is that the same as a goal?" I asked.

"No. A goal is different. A goal is not a purpose. A goal is something tangible. It is something definite you can accomplish. It has a beginning and an end. A purpose is ongoing. It gives meaning and definition to our lives. Living by your word—doing what you say you're going to do—or raising responsible children could be examples of purposes. You see, a purpose is a particular road you choose to travel. A goal is one of the places you intend to visit on that road. For example, a goal can be to make money, but would you feel comfortable with that as your purpose in life? Would you like the epitaph chiseled on your tombstone to be your average salary for your last five working years?"

"Of course not," I replied.

"So while making money is a goal we can strive for, it is not our purpose in life, although many people act as if it is. Purpose is bigger. It is the picture you have of yourself—the kind of person you want to be or the kind of life you want to lead. It's like your own personal mission statement."

"It sounds as if your purpose is almost like trying to decide what kind of business you are in as a person."

"That's a nice way of putting it."

"Is one's attitude toward ethics and morality part of one's purpose?" I asked.

"It should be," said the advisor. "There is a much higher chance that you will do the morally right thing if being ethical is part of your purpose—that is, if you picture yourself as an ethical person."

"If you have a purpose, how do you stick to it?" I asked. "We all know that 'the road to hell is paved with good intentions.'"

"Sticking to one's purpose is what I call being *right with life*—behaving in a way that makes you feel good about yourself day in and day out. One of the best ways I know to help you stick to your purpose is to use the mirror test."

"The what?"

"The mirror test. Can you look at yourself in the mirror without guilt? When you do what's right, you can look yourself straight in the eye. But when you disregard your purpose and do something that you know is wrong, you won't feel good about yourself. No matter how much you rationalize your actions, you will feel uncomfortable."

The advisor then handed me a card. "This poem called 'The Man in the Glass' will say it better than I can. An old friend of mine, Lowell Thomas, gave it to me one day after one of my talks. He said, 'Frankly, if you had read this poem, your talk would have been much better.' I keep it in my wallet and refer to it frequently. For a long time I thought this verse was anonymous, but recently I learned that it was the work of a man named Dale Wimbrow. He wrote it some time ago, so the language may sound sexist, but the message is still valid for all of us."

THE MAN IN THE GLASS

BY
DALE WIMBROW

When you get what you want in your struggle for self
    And the world makes you king for a day,
Just go to a mirror and look at yourself
    And see what THAT man has to say.

For it isn't your father or mother or wife
    Whose judgment upon you must pass;
The fellow whose verdict counts most in your life
    Is the one staring back from the glass.

Some people may think you a straight-shootin' chum
    And call you a wonderful guy,
But the man in the glass says you're only a bum
    If you can't look him straight in the eye.

He's the fellow to please, never mind all the rest,
    For he's with you clear up to the end.
And you've passed your most dangerous, difficult test
    If the man in the glass is your friend.

You may fool the whole world down the pathway of life
    And get pats on your back as you pass,
But your final reward will be heartaches and tears
    If you've cheated the man in the glass.

"**T**HAT poem makes your message very clear," I said. "But don't some people do the wrong thing and then rationalize what they did so that they feel it was actually the right thing to do?"

"Yes, many people do that," said the advisor, "but if they take a good hard look at themselves, down deep they know they have done wrong. If you go against your image of yourself and what you think is right, you can't help but feel bad. It's counter to your purpose—the picture you have of yourself as an ethical person."

"So a clear purpose is the foundation upon which sound ethical behavior is built," I said. "What's the second principle of ethical power?"

"Pride," said the advisor. "What I mean by pride in this context is the sense of satisfaction that you get from your accomplishments as well as those of the people you care about, like your family or staff. To hold to your purpose, you must believe in yourself and have faith in your abilities. I'm convinced that people who have a healthy amount of self-esteem tend to have the strength to do what they know is right—even when there are strong pressures to do otherwise. You certainly wouldn't have done what you did recently if you didn't have significant self-esteem."

"Then self-esteem is a key factor to leading an ethical life," I said. "It seemed to me that the most powerful Ethics Check question was 'How will it make me feel about myself?'"

"Self-esteem is very important," said the advisor. "It is healthy and justified to feel good about yourself and your accomplishments. That's what pride is all about. Some people, however, have too much or too little pride. A sense of inferiority or inadequacy often plays itself out in one of two ways, either of which can impact upon your ethical behavior: false pride or self-doubt."

"What do you mean by 'false pride'?"

"False pride is a negative kind of pride that occurs when people have a distorted image of their own importance. They think they deserve *all* the credit, that they are the source of *all* good ideas, that their work is *the most important,* that they don't need the help of others, and so on."

"When that happens, I imagine you start to get a big head and let your ego get in your way," I said.

"That's for sure," said the advisor. "Nothing can get us off course quicker than false pride—it blurs our purpose. What you want," he said thoughtfully, "is pride sprinkled with a fair amount of humility. Remember:

*

People
With
Humility
Don't
Think
Less
Of
Themselves . . .

They
Just
Think
About
Themselves
Less

*

"People with false pride," continued the advisor, "tend to regard themselves as the center of all things. They develop a big 'I,' little 'you' perspective toward others. Consequently, every difference of opinion they encounter becomes a win-lose confrontation. Their constant need to win can motivate them to rationalize, cover up, exaggerate, argue, and lie when they are in the wrong. They'll do anything to avoid looking bad. Their pride can't allow losing and their egos go out of control."

"I've known a number of people like that," I said. "In fact, my boss fits your description perfectly. He'd do anything to achieve our sales quota because he's afraid of looking bad. 'Expediency' is his middle name. That's why I didn't go to him for advice. He always needs to be right, even when it's obvious to everyone else that he isn't. Even a casual conversation with him seems competitive. I've often said I wouldn't want to be him. Needing to be right all the time has to be an exhausting way to live."

"Also lonely, because pride always separates," continued the advisor. "When the desire to be right or take all the credit rules your life, it separates you from your true self, from others, and from any possible spiritual growth. When we think we have a lock on the perfect answer or the only correct interpretation of the facts, we can easily become defensive and cut ourselves off from vital feedback, which can produce valuable new ideas and suggestions from others."

"It sounds like my boss again," I said. "All of his people—myself and the other sales managers— have stopped giving him feedback or suggestions because whenever we do, he yells at us. After getting verbally beaten up a few times, we have learned to keep our opinions to ourselves."

"That's pathetic, isn't it?" sighed the advisor. "But, unfortunately, it's typical of many managers."

"You mentioned self-doubt earlier," I said. "How's that different from false pride?"

"People with self-doubt usually don't like themselves very much and they don't trust their own judgment. As a result, they are driven by a desire to be liked and accepted by others. They don't want to make waves or stand out in the crowd. Therefore, it can be more difficult for these people to be morally strong because they have trouble standing up against pressure from others."

"So people with self-doubt listen to others too much and people with false pride listen to others too little," I concluded.

"Yes," said the advisor. "In terms of their daily behavior, people who have self-doubt view themselves as *'worth-less'* than others, while people with false pride view themselves as *'worth-more'* than others. And both behavior patterns are the result of feelings of inferiority, or a lack of self-esteem."

"I can understand that self-doubt comes from lack of self-esteem, but I find it hard to believe that false pride is also a result of low self-esteem. I always thought of people like my boss as having an inflated ego."

"When I first realized this characteristic of human nature I was surprised, too," replied the advisor. "But the more I observed the phenomenon, the more I realized that people who act as if only *they* count and others don't count at all are really trying to make up for their own 'I-don't-count' feelings. You see, we all need affirmation—a pat on the back, an 'atta boy' or 'atta girl' at appropriate times—particularly, when we're young.

"If we don't get enough recognition," continued the advisor, "we become seemingly unrecognizable to ourselves and begin to think everyone is against us. It's like a TV documentary I saw the other night about crime. I was surprised to see that the criminals profiled were operating on the belief that 'you better get them before they get you.' When people are overly aggressive or hostile, it's hard to remember that deep down they probably feel like victims. Animals often go on the attack when they are scared. So do people. If they don't feel good about themselves, people often overcompensate for those 'not OK' feelings by moving out into the world and trying to control everything and everybody."

"I get the impression that how we are brought up has a tremendous impact on how we feel about ourselves," I remarked.

"Absolutely," replied the advisor. "If you grow up in a home where praise, encouragement, and caring are the rule, then you are more likely to learn to appreciate and to respect others, and to have confidence in yourself. And confidence in yourself gives you the strength to make good ethical decisions despite pressure to act otherwise."

"That's true at work as well as at home," I said. "I now understand that self-esteem and pride are *learned* attitudes."

"Yes," continued the advisor. "And it is equally important to understand that inferiority and self-doubt can be *unlearned*."

"How do I do that?"

"Several ways. First start by affirming yourself. Stop putting yourself down. If you're not for yourself, who will be?"

"So I should be my own best friend?"

"Absolutely," said the advisor. "Second, seek out and gather people around you who support and encourage you. Avoid individuals who are negative or always putting you down. These kinds of people are parasites who drain you of your inner strength. And don't be awestruck by other people or feel you have to compete against them. Remember, no one can be you as effectively as yourself; but try to be your *best* self."

"Any other suggestions?" I asked with a smile.

"Well, since you asked," chuckled the advisor, "this may sound simple, but it's not always easy to do: *Choose to feel good about yourself.* People often don't realize that this choice is up to them. I firmly believe the saying *'God did not make junk.'* The Almighty gave people the freedom to choose and, unfortunately, some people *choose* to junk up their lives. We must take responsibility for the condition we're in and stop acting like passive victims. You may not have had much control in shaping your current circumstances, but you have the power to change your circumstances and thereby shape your future. Once you realize this fact, a lot of anger and frustration wash away.

"Every day you have two choices," continued the advisor. "You can choose to feel good about yourself, or you can choose to feel lousy. Why choose the latter? One of my favorite sayings is attributed to Eleanor Roosevelt:

*

*No One
Can
Make
You Feel
Inferior
Without
Your
Permission*

*

"**S**O THE idea is to build up your own self-esteem and pride," I said, "but not to get carried away with your own importance."

"That's it exactly," smiled the advisor. "What we all need is a strong sense of *balance*. If we have balance, we will have the self-confidence to hang tough when confronted by difficult ethical situations."

"I think I have a good understanding of the power of true self-esteem," I said. "What is the third principle of ethical power?"

"*Patience,*" said the advisor. "Once we have a clear purpose and our ego is under control, the third principle necessary for sound ethical behavior is patience. One reason why people sometimes get off course is because they lack faith; and with lack of faith, they become impatient."

"Are you talking about spiritual faith?"

"Yes, that's a *part* of it," the advisor emphasized, "but also faith in a more general sense. Positive thinking is another aspect of faith. It is the energized belief that no matter what happens, things are going to work out all right because we can handle whatever happens. This faith is *not* resignation—nor is it the mere acceptance of something, like when we say, 'OK, I buy that. I believe that.' We have faith when we believe in something and we base our actions, indeed our whole life, on that belief. On the other hand, when we lack faith we tend to grab for the here and now. In so doing, we sabotage the future."

"What do you mean by 'sabotage the future'?"

"There's a story from my childhood that illustrates the point," said the advisor. "When I was about five years old I saw the movie *Jack and the Beanstalk* and decided to grow my own beanstalk where we were living.

"The next morning," he continued, "I took a fresh lima bean from my mom's groceries and planted it in our backyard. I watered it carefully and waited for something to happen. After two days I became anxious to see results, so I dug up the bean to see how it was doing. Needless to say, it wasn't doing much. I continued to replant the bean and then dig it up every day for a week. I became so frustrated with the lack of progress that I finally dug up the bean and *stomped* on it!

"People often do the same sort of thing when trying to make an ethical decision," said the advisor. "They don't trust the process. They make what they think is a sound decision but they want immediate reassurance that they did the right thing. They become impatient. Lacking faith in their own judgment, they undo what, in the long run, would have been the best decision."

"It's difficult to have patience in today's world of instant gratification," I said. "Your point reminds me that I must have confidence in my decision not to hire our competitor's salesperson. Otherwise, I'll keep second-guessing myself and eventually undo a good decision."

"You're right about patience being especially difficult today," replied the advisor. "And it's precisely because of the fast pace of our world that we so desperately need to rediscover the importance of faith and to take a long-range view of the consequences of our actions."

"Sounds as if you're saying we need to get the Big Picture." I smiled. "Do you have a simple solution for that too?"

"The first step"—he nodded with a knowing smile—"is to become aware of a more universal timing, which may or may not be the same as your own."

"That reminds me of the movie *Oh, God!,* when John Denver asks George Burns, 'Did you really create the world in six days, and rest on the seventh?'

"George Burns in the role of God said, 'Yes, I did, but you'll have to remember my days are a little longer than yours. When I got up this morning, Freud was in medical school.'"

"That speaks precisely to a more universal timing," agreed the advisor. "The belief that there is something greater than ourselves. I call it God, while others call it spirituality or a higher power.

"A successful business friend expressed this well to me one day," he continued. "He said that once he learned to be patient and trust the timing of a higher power, he noticed that things began to work out for him. If he needed an answer to a problem by, say, nine o'clock Thursday morning, he'd find that he might not get the answer on Monday, Tuesday, or Wednesday. But if he definitely had to have the solution by nine o'clock Thursday, he would receive it. When he didn't, he discovered that it really wasn't necessary after all. In other words, when he needed it, he got it. Things always worked out."

"It sounds as if when you have patience," I said, "you have a different way of looking at things. You don't have to always have things right *now*."

"That's right," cheered the advisor. "The negative side effect of impatience—of having to have things happen *now*—is a possible poor decision. When you have patience, you realize that if you do what is right—even if it costs you in the short run—it will pay off in the long run. Remember:

*

*Nice Guys
May Appear
To Finish
Last,
But
Usually
They're
Running
In A
Different
Race*

*

"Now that you mention it," I said, "a friend who is an art director at a magazine is a perfect example of a 'nice guy' who eventually won. He was fired for refusing to do something he thought was wrong. He was asked by his boss to direct a project that included what he considered to be pornographic material. After a lot of agonizing, he declined to do the assignment, and as a result he was dismissed. After that, he had a difficult time finding a new job. Even his kids had to get jobs after school to help out. Finally, almost a year later, he was offered a great job—even better than the one he had left. The irony was he clinched the new job as a result of his old boss's recommendation!"

"So even though his previous manager had fired him, your friend had earned his respect?"

"Y ES. So patience paid off for him," I said. "I sure hope it can do the same for me. What's the fourth principle of ethical power?"

"Persistence," exclaimed the advisor with a big gesture. "Stick-to-itiveness! I don't know whether that's a word, but that's what it's all about. Patience is necessary, but without persistence, it's not sufficient to keep you on track. I'll never forget the story about the speech Winston Churchill gave in his late years at an English prep school he had attended as a boy. The headmaster told the boys, 'This is an historic moment. Winston Churchill is the greatest speaker of the English language. Write down everything he says. He will make an unforgettable speech!' When Churchill walked out to give his speech, he peered over the top of his glasses and said:

*

Never!
Never!
Never!
Never!
Give Up!

*

"With that," continued the advisor, "Churchill sat down. Many students were disappointed, but the headmaster, upon reflection, felt this might have been one of Churchill's greatest speeches because it summarized a lifetime of thinking. If one quality epitomized Winston Churchill, it was persistence. He never gave up. It was that attitude that inspired England in World War II to continue to fight when others might have surrendered. In terms of ethical behavior, persistence means sticking to your guns. It's keeping your commitment and making your actions consistent with your guiding principles."

"So if I believe I am an ethical person—someone who knows right from wrong—then I need to consistently act in a way that lives up to my mental image."

"That's it," said the advisor. "Being an ethical person means behaving ethically *all the time*—not only when it's convenient. In fact, it is especially important to act ethically when it is inconvenient or unpopular to do so. We need to make a distinction between commitment and interest. When you are interested in doing something you do it only when it's convenient. Often there is an excuse for why you can't do what you said you would do. When you are committed to do something, however, you accept no excuses—only results."

"So when you talk about persistence," I said, "you're not talking about *trying* to do something. You're talking about actually *doing* it."

"Absolutely," said the advisor. "I always say:

*

Trying
Is
Just
A
Noisy
Way
Of
Not
Doing
Something

*

"Unfortunately, that hits close to home," I said.

"So many people make all kinds of noise about doing something with hardly any follow-up action."

"That's true," said the advisor. "When you're committed, you find ways to suppress your rationalizations. Even when it's inconvenient you keep to your moral commitment. Persistence in life is characterized by this ethical toughness."

"That's a valuable distinction to make," I said. "In my recent dilemma with that salesperson, I could have told myself, 'This is not the time to be ethical. This guy can really make a difference to our bottom line.' I could have been, as you say, interested in doing what was right, but not committed to doing it."

"Ray Kroc, the founder of McDonald's, had a framed message on his wall he often showed visitors," continued the advisor. Reaching into his desk, the advisor produced a copy.

Nothing can take
the place of
persistence.

Talent will not;
nothing is more common
than unsuccessful men
with great talent.

Genius will not;
unrewarded genius is
almost a proverb.

Education will not;
the world is full of
educated derelicts.

Persistence and
determination
alone are omnipotent.

"IF IT won't reveal my age too much," grinned the advisor, "that's an adaptation of a quote originally attributed to Calvin Coolidge. He always felt if all people would do the few simple things they knew they ought to do, most of our big problems would take care of themselves."

"The headline is," I said, "that I must have persistence to stick to my purpose and to achieve what I envision. If I keep my vision clearly and frequently in mind, it will become reality. I understand. What's the fifth principle of ethical power?"

"The fifth principle is *Perspective*," he said. "Perspective is the capacity to see what is *really* important in any given situation. That is why I illustrate the five principles as a wheel with perspective as the hub around which the other four P's rotate."

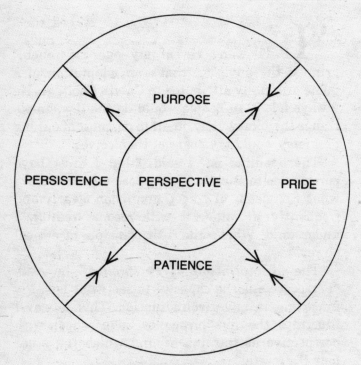

The Interrelationship Between the Five P's

I said, "It looks as if perspective is the central place from which you can oversee the other four principles."

"That's a good way of putting it," agreed the advisor. "Unfortunately, most people are so busy doing what they call 'living' that they don't take the time to seek a peaceful moment when they can find their own special place from which to view their lives. It is because of this lack of perspective that their lives are out of balance and they never seem to be fulfilled."

"How does one find that balance and sense of fulfillment?" I wondered aloud.

"By waking up your *inner* self, each and every single new morning." I looked puzzled, so the advisor continued. "First, you must realize that each of us has two selves. There's our external self, which is task-oriented; its attention is outward, focused on getting things done. Then, there's our inner self, which is more inward— reflective and thoughtful; its attention is on meaning and values, on finding significance in life. This inner self takes longer to wake up in the morning than our external self. As a result, most people don't even know it's there; they leap out of bed and are right into their busy task-oriented selves, doing their daily routines, before their inner selves have awakened."

"You've got me pegged," I smiled. "The minute I'm on my feet in the morning I'm off and running. I turn on the radio or TV, brush my teeth, get the coffeepot going, run around looking for clean clothes to wear, shower, read the newspaper—I doubt if my inner self gets a chance to wake up at all! Do you use any special method to wake up your inner self?"

"Some people pray," said the advisor, "others meditate, write in a journal, or do devotional reading and contemplation; others practice yoga, listen to music, walk or run, bicycle or swim. The important thing is that you get yourself in a reflective state."

"There's no one 'best way' to enter your day?"

"No," said the advisor. "But it always involves an inner quieting of the mind. Also, it is best achieved in solitude. Time alone is tough for busy, involved people to find. It's the price they pay for success. It may mean having to set the alarm earlier. My wife and I have a time each morning we call 'being alone together.' We sit quietly in prayer and thoughtful meditation, read together, or share an inspirational thought. I also walk two or three miles a day. Walks are good times for reflection."

"So you do a variety of things," I said. "I wish I could do even one of those things on a regular basis, but I just don't have the time. To put that program into effect, I'd need more time."

The advisor came right back at me, "You have all the time there is."

"What do you mean?"

"There are exactly twenty-four hours in each day. You have to manage within that fixed limit. Let me use an analogy. Suppose you are playing chess and your opponent says, 'Checkmate!' He or she has you cornered and the game is over. You can't say, 'I want more board!'"

I laughed at the idea.

"Yet you are asking for something like that when you say you need more time," continued the advisor. "Managing your time isn't the real issue. Your time is fixed. What you need is to manage the activities that are consuming your time."

"How can I do that?"

"By not letting your appointment calendar manage *you*," the advisor replied. "For example, when someone calls and asks you to do something, don't automatically go to your calendar to see if you have time. Instead, reflect on your purpose and related goals and ask yourself if you really want to commit your time to that person or activity in the first place. If you consistently do this, it will be easier to keep yourself on track and live according to your purpose, values, and ethical beliefs."

"Sounds as if the key is to let my purpose and goals drive my behavior. Maybe the next time I ask myself 'Whose life is this anyway?' I can honestly answer 'MINE!'" I laughed again. "I see how I can really start to feel that I'm in charge of what happens to me instead of always reacting to pressures of the world around me."

"Precisely," the advisor said, "and to have a fulfilling life, you must take time to maintain balance in your life or you will be cheating yourself. When that balance is present, it allows us to live a more ethically principled life-style consistent with our purpose in life. Do you know why most people come to me for advice? It's because they have become so busy with the 'business' of their lives—the routine mechanics of their schedules—that they have lost touch with what it's all for, what their lives are truly all about."

"I can understand that," I said. "So enough quiet time each day, preferably in the morning, to reflect and get things in perspective is a must. Do you ever take longer periods of time for reflection?" I asked.

"Periodically," said the advisor. "Red Scott, a corporation president I respect a great deal, has an interesting approach to the subject of reflection.

"Red tells a story about his first career change. At the time he had a very good job in Dallas. But he received an attractive offer to move to New York City and work on Wall Street. Having spent no time at all in the Big Apple, he was not sure what to do.

"He remembered having met a man named Julian Bobo, who had enjoyed great success in the securities industry in Dallas and who was something of a local legend. Red called Mr. Bobo and explained the situation.

"Mr. Bobo said, 'Red, I'd be happy to give you advice but only under one condition—that you do exactly what I say. Now you might not want to do that, so why don't you think about it and call me back.'

"Since Red had nowhere else to turn for expert advice, he called back and agreed to do exactly as Mr. Bobo advised.

"Mr. Bobo told Red to go to New York and talk to the people offering him the job. But, he said, he wanted Red to travel in a very special way. He was to go by train—a couple of days' journey from Dallas. He was to rent a private compartment. He was not to take anything to read, listen to, or write with on the trip. He was to talk to no one but the porter or the dining-car waiters. When Red got to New York City, he was to call Mr. Bobo immediately, who would then tell him exactly what to do next.

"Reluctantly, Red followed Mr. Bobo's orders to the letter. The first few hours he stared out of the train window at the scenery. But after a while, that became totally boring. Since he had nothing to read or listen to and was unable to write, and couldn't talk with anybody, he began to think. He thought about people he knew and places he'd been. He thought about things he had done and things he wanted to do. On the second day he realized that what he was doing was exactly what Mr. Bobo wanted him to do—to think and to reflect. A few hours before the train reached New York City he finally broke one of Mr. Bobo's rules. He asked the porter for a pencil and some paper.

"Red wrote down a carefully worded statement of his major purpose in life as well as a brief list of his goals. His decision was clear.

"When he got off the train he went to a phone, called Mr. Bobo as agreed, and said, 'I know now that you wanted me to think things through for myself. I've done that, and I want you to know that my decision is clear to me now. I don't need any further advice, and I really want to thank you for what you've done.'

"Mr. Bobo laughed and said, 'I didn't think you would need me anymore.'

"Red took the New York City job and it launched him on a very successful career. Ever since then, he has taken a couple of days off almost every year, just to reflect. Sometimes he rents a cabin in the mountains where there are no phones, no TV sets, and no other distractions. One year he took another train ride. Last year he went to the seashore and walked on the beach. After careful reflection, he writes down those things he most values, and then his own personal goals, as well as goals for his company. He finds this time alone for thinking to be invaluable. It keeps him 'on purpose.' Upon reflection, Red says, difficult problems become much less complicated."

"So taking time to be by yourself and reflect in solitude can actually help you be more effective."

"There is no question about it," said my advisor. "I am continually amazed at how clear my thinking becomes afterward, particularly if I'm faced with a big problem. It's as if the answer I am seeking exists somewhere already, just waiting for me to tune in to it. The solitude, quiet, and reflection are the tuning-in process.

"And so, a core belief I have is that:

*

Every
Problem
Can Be
Solved
If
You Take
Some Quiet Time
To Reflect,
Seek Guidance,
And
Put Things
Into
Perspective

*

"Reflecting may seem like daydreaming, but it's really very practical. The key is to find a way to achieve serenity and to listen for guidance from within. That gives me perspective, and when I can achieve perspective my purpose becomes increasingly clear."

"So perspective brings us full circle back to our purpose," I said.

"It sure does," smiled the advisor. "Here's something to help you remember the Five Principles of Ethical Power," he added as he handed me a small card.

*The Five Principles of Ethical Power
for Individuals*

1. **Purpose:** I see myself as being an ethically sound person. I let my conscience be my guide. No matter what happens, I am always able to face the mirror, look myself straight in the eye, and feel good about myself.

2. **Pride:** I feel good about myself. I don't need the acceptance of other people to feel important. A balanced self-esteem keeps my ego and my desire to be accepted from influencing my decisions.

3. **Patience:** I believe that things will eventually work out well. I don't need everything to happen right now. I am at peace with what comes my way!

4. **Persistence:** I stick to my purpose, especially when it seems inconvenient to do so! My behavior is consistent with my intentions. As Churchill said, "Never! Never! Never! Never! Give up!"

5. **Perspective:** I take time to enter each day quietly in a mood of reflection. This helps me to get myself focused and allows me to listen to my inner self and to see things more clearly.

"**I** URGE you to keep the card handy," said my advisor as I thanked him for his invaluable advice and we said good-bye to each other.

Over the next several months I began to share what I had learned. Using the Ethics Check became common practice in my division. And everyone learned and started to talk about the Five Principles of Ethical Power. I was also able to find another highly qualified sales representative to fill my open position. He seemed to be ethical and more than willing to fit in with the new direction I had planned for our division.

I even made some changes in my daily routine. For example, I began to take time each morning to enter my day more calmly. An early-morning walk became a ritual along with moments for quiet reflection. I started a journal to record my thoughts.

As a result of these changes, if I ran into a difficult situation during the day I was better equipped to sort out the truly important issues. Taking the time to reflect brought my purpose into focus. When I looked in the mirror I felt good about myself.

What was eye-opening, however, was the number of times my ego got in the way. My false pride was stronger than I had thought. I'll admit that I didn't bat a 1,000, but referring to the Five Principles of Ethical Power helped me make better decisions and make them more quickly.

Even my patience improved. "It will all work out," I heard myself saying time and again.

AND "persistence" became one of my favorite words. When I said I was going to do something, I really did it. Even my wife and kids started calling me "old reliable."

However, as I began to feel better about myself, one thing still disturbed me—the seeming lack of support in my company for ethical decision-making.

What became clear was the number of mixed messages we received. While the chairman of the board made public statements about ethics and morality, questionable actions of many in our company spoke louder than his words. It seemed a long way from the executive suite to the front lines of sales.

As a middle manager I felt particularly vulnerable. I was caught in the middle of this double standard. I knew many other managers at my level felt the same way. While everyone I talked to professed to believe in fair play and sound ethics, in reality their good intentions were lost under the pressure to get the job done and get ahead. Goal accomplishment was seen as all important—with the ends often justifying the means, whether ethical or not. People like me, who tried to act ethically, were often considered part of the problem rather than part of the solution, and we were being treated accordingly.

IN recent years our company had been facing stiffer competition from abroad. In addition, we had entered some tough, newly deregulated markets. The response to these competitive pressures was to set lofty goals at the top; but by the time they got to my level, they took on the appearance of threats.

Recently, in fact, a middle manager was fired and several of his junior managers demoted after years of successful and loyal service because their division lost money on a single contract. As a result, I found case after case where fundamentally honest managers felt driven to unethical acts in order to produce desired bottom-line results that protected them from this kind of harsh treatment. This was particularly true when they had been pressured to set goals that were unrealistic.

For me, this all resurfaced as the million-dollar question: *Is it possible today to stay competitive in business and still operate in an honest and ethical manner?*

While I did not have a clear answer to my own question, I knew it was a very important one because the answer had tremendous implications for how emloyees are treated and how they feel about where they work. When people feel negative toward their company, they often look for ways to "even things out"—like calling in sick when they aren't sick at all, making personal long-distance telephone calls, padding expense accounts, taking office supplies home, snitching product samples, and many other questionable actions that may not seem like serious offenses but in the aggregate become a serious problem.

I read recently that a top manager from a major retail chain said he could reduce prices to customers 20 percent if he could stop employee theft. I began to realize that business organizations can either foster sound ethical decision-making or retard it.

What I had learned was helping me to determine what I personally should do, but I was wondering what strategies organizations and managers could use. So I phoned the advisor again.

"**Y**OU'RE right," he responded. "There are ways in which companies can encourage and foster management decisions grounded in ethics. But managing people at work is not my field. However, I have a friend who is a business consultant, who has worked with companies all over the world. You should talk to him."

The next afternoon when I arrived at the consultant's office, I found a smiling, neatly dressed man in his mid-forties. He had the warm demeanor and style of a self-assured man.

As we sat down, he asked, "I understand you are interested in business ethics?"

"Yes," I replied. "Your advisor friend agreed with me that organizations can actually create an environment conducive to ethical behavior. I have observed people in my company who are stealing or lying, or cheating and covering up—things I believe they wouldn't ordinarily do outside the company environment. When they are at work, they often seem to feel justified in behaving differently. What I want to know is, 'How can I help the company turn this situation around?'"

"Every manager can play an important role in helping his or her organization to create the kind of positive and productive environment that fosters sound ethical decision-making and behavior," he answered. "The more I work with organizations, the more I am convinced that it all comes down to how people—both employees and customers—perceive the way they are being treated by the organization and its management.

"**M**Y dream is that some day there will be companies designated as the 'Fortunate 500,'" continued the consultant.

"The *Fortunate* 500?"

"Yes," said the consultant. "Size would not be the main criterion for membership. 'Fortunate 500' companies would be profitable, but would also place a high emphasis on such factors as the quality of life available to employees and the quality of services given to customers."

"'Fortunate 500' companies. I like that concept. Could the 'Fortunate 500' list include nonprofit organizations from education, government, medicine, the military, religion, or even voluntary enterprises?" I asked.

"Why not?" replied the consultant. "As long as they were organizations that were accomplishing their goals, treating people well, and were practicing the Five Principles of Ethical Power."

"So you think the Five P's that I learned from the advisor apply to organizations too."

"Absolutely," said the consultant. "*Purpose* in organizations is the vision of the organization communicated from the top. Conditions in business today require the emergence of a new leadership with high principles. In fact, I recently read that in an extensive survey asking people to describe the most desirable leadership qualities, the most frequently mentioned attribute by far was 'integrity.'

"So business should get away from its wheeler-dealer image in which you do anything to get results and beat the competition."

"Yes," said the consultant. "This new leadership has to create a positive, productive, and ethically grounded environment. When I was in Japan a few years ago I heard the eighty-eight-year-old chairman of the board of Matsushita Electric speak."

"Just a kid," I joked.

"Right," said the consultant. "One of the executives I was with asked him, 'Sir, what is your primary job as chairman of the board of this great international company?'

"He didn't hesitate. He said, 'To model love. I am the *soul* of this company. It is through me that our organization's values pass.'"

The soul of the company! It was a startling concept to me.

"I liked the answer," said the consultant. "It reminded me of a parable called 'The Lost Soul,' written by Jan Abbott. It's the story of a vice-president who searches for his lost soul. One day as he is firing an employee, the employee says, 'I hope someday you'll find your soul again.' Then the employee stands up and leaves.

"The vice-president thinks to himself, 'That's a funny thing for someone to say. Come to think of it, though, I haven't seen my soul for awhile.'

"Now when something was lost, the vice-president always reported it to Lost and Found. So he calls and asks, 'Have you seen my soul?' The secretary says, 'We don't handle lost souls. I recommend you talk to the security officer. He's the expert on lost souls.'

"When he contacts the security officer, the man says, 'This is a serious problem. Why don't you come down so we can talk.'"

"When the vice-president goes to see the security officer, the first question he is asked is 'Can you remember when you used your soul last?' The vice-president says, 'No. That's my problem.'

"After some more discussion, the vice-president suddenly perks up and says, 'Maybe I left it in the president's office.'

"'Ah-ha!' says the security officer. 'I knew it. You'd be surprised how often that happens. I'm a specialist in soul recovery and I'd say that is one of the most common things that happens to souls. Why don't we go down to the boss's office and ask if he has seen it.'

"When they get to the president's office, the security officer says to the president, 'We've got a serious problem. The vice-president here has lost his soul. Have you seen it?'

"The president blurts out, 'What on earth would I want with a soul? Very undesirable in business. Souls get in the way of clear thinking. Make people soft. We need hard-nosed managers around here. Competition is too tough for souls. It took me a long time to get rid of mine. Frankly,' he says to the vice-president, 'I didn't know you had one. If I were you, I wouldn't worry about losing it. You're doing fine without it—just the type of manager I like.

"'By the way,' the president says to the vice-president, 'how is that presentation for the corporate people coming along? Make sure the figures come out right, won't you? We don't want to upset them.'

"As they are leaving, the security officer turns to the vice-president and says, 'Do you still want to find your soul? I didn't get the impression just now that souls are valued much around here.'

"'Yes, now more than ever,' says the vice-president. 'Do you have any suggestions?'

"'To find your soul,' answers the security officer, 'we'll have to determine when you used it last. Why don't I send out an interoffice memo and ask if anyone can recall seeing your soul in action lately.'

"'Hey, I don't want to admit to everybody that I don't have a soul,' says the vice-president.

"'Why not?' asks the security officer. 'The president didn't even know you had one.'

"The security officer sends out a memo. On the day's first shift no one replies. The vice-president is disappointed. Then during the second shift an employee finally comes forward who says he has seen the vice-president's soul in action. 'Last year you hit my car in the parking garage and you went through a lot of trouble to track me down. If you hadn't done that, there would have been no way that I could have discovered who damaged my car.'

"After the man leaves, the security officer says, 'That's great. Honesty is a good place to start any soul-recovery program.'

"So, starting with honesty," said the consultant, "the vice-president finally gets his soul back. When he thanks the security officer, he says, 'I don't think the president is going to be pleased with my presentation. Now that I've got my soul back, I'm not going to tinker with the figures. And they aren't good this quarter. The corporate people won't be happy.'"

"That's a thought-provoking story," I said.

"The reason I like it," said the consultant, "is because in a very simple way it says so much. What good ethical behavior comes down to is *soul* —where you house your values, your purpose in life, including the picture of the kind of person you want to be. Without your soul you have nothing to guide you. In an organization, the soul should be represented by top management and their hopes, visions, and purpose for the enterprise."

"Could this be expressed through your mission statement and possibly a Code of Ethics and Standards of Conduct policy?" I asked.

"Yes, those are excellent ways to communicate purpose in a business organization and to set out the values and beliefs of the company's leadership."

"Do you know of any good examples of ethical leadership from top management?"

"Yes," said the consultant. "I hear good stories every day. I know there are many more managers who provide sound ethical leadership than there are scoundrels and cheats. Because we don't make them heroes, we just don't hear much about them. Honest and decent people who know the power of ethical management have to come out of hiding.

"I just heard a great example of ethical leadership from a top manager in the hotel business," continued the consultant. "She told me how, following her husband's death, she found herself in charge of their company. The organization was not in very good shape. Lack of ethics and low morale were the main reasons why. Cheating, lying, and stealing had become widespread. Because her husband had been ill a long time, there was no longer clear leadership at the top. So she and her son, whom she appointed president, began to turn the situation around.

"They didn't do anything very sophisticated. They just put one foot in front of the other, and followed their instincts. As the top managers of the company, they started to talk to the middle managers and employees very honestly and openly about ethics. They told all their employees: 'We might not always agree with you, but we always want you to be open and honest with us. In return, we promise to listen to you and not to deceive you in any way.' They set honesty and truth as the cornerstones of their hotel-management approach.

"In two years the turnaround has been fantastic. Not only has morale increased dramatically as the employees realized that top management cared, but things that had been major problems, like employee theft, have decreased significantly. As she related, 'We even had a maid come to us with almost $1,000 in loose cash she had found left behind by a hotel guest in a bureau drawer.

"'And, as she gave us the $1,000, the maid said, "Two years ago I wouldn't have done this." It was another three or four days before the guest realized he might have left the money in the drawer and frantically called about it. Much to his amazement, we had the money for him.'"

"What happened to the maid?" I asked. "Did they reward her?"

"They didn't give her any monetary reward at the time, but her story was well publicized throughout the company, as well as in the local media. I understand she has been recently promoted to supervisor.

"My hotel manager friend and her son try to show people that when they do things that are ethically sound and right, they gain a 'psychic income' from management—their actions are noticed and praised and they are appreciated."

"Stories like that should be more widely publicized," I said. "Do you have any other examples of ethical leadership from the top?"

"Yes," said the consultant. "Another manager I respect heads up a mechanical contracting company. He tells his employees that they will always have a job with him as long as they do not lie to him or steal, even if there is no work for a period of time. He says, 'My people and I are in this together, and if they are honest with me, I will be committed to them. We have a spirit of genuine mutual trust. We'll figure out something to get through tough times together.'"

"What if an employee is honest but incompetent?" I asked. "Would he keep that person?"

"First, the manager would accept responsibility for creating such a situation," said the consultant. "After all, he hired this person. Second, he would do everything possible to train and work with this person until the right position for the individual is found in the company. If that is not possible, he will help the person find a suitable career in some other organization through a sincere, committed outplacement program. He wants all his people to win even if the only way to do that is to have them leave his organization."

"Is his company profitable?"

"**Y**ES," said the consultant. "Very profitable, and he has survived some really bad times. The way he treats his employees is reflected in the quality of their work and how they treat their customers."

"I now see how purpose plays a role in a company," I said. "If you don't have a clear vision of what you want the company to be, it is apt to become something you don't want. When there are no standards for behavior, anything goes. Tell me about pride in organizations."

"*Pride* in organizations is a reflection of how people feel about the organization they work for," said the consultant. *"I'm convinced that people's negative feelings about their organization are at the root of unethical behavior.*

"If people feel appreciated," continued the consultant, "they are more likely to resist temptation to act unethically. If they are proud of their company and what it represents, people will fight to maintain integrity in the organization. When that occurs, it is proof that the organization's purpose or mission is working on a daily basis."

"How do you generate that kind of organizational pride?"

"I think it starts from the inside and moves out," said the consultant. "Before they can have pride in their organization, people must first feel good about themselves and what they are doing for the company. As Benjamin Franklin reportedly once said:

*

You
Can't
Expect
An Empty Bag
To
Stand
Up
Straight

*

"In other words, you must help people build up their self-esteem before you can expect them to be strong," I said.

"Exactly," said the consultant. "And you build up self-esteem by accentuating positive experiences. It's like making deposits into a bank account. Every time you have a positive interaction with somebody, for example, and you catch that person doing something right and praise him or her, it's like putting money in their self-esteem account. If you and that person are able to make enough positive deposits, when the going gets tough and that person needs inner strength to draw upon, there is something in the account. However, if that person has not built up a reserve of good feelings about himself or herself, there is nothing to draw upon to resist pressures to behave unethically."

"I like the concept of catching people doing things right. Most organizations are set up to accentuate the negative and to catch people doing things wrong rather than right, aren't they? Our company certainly is guilty of that."

"That's very true of most workplaces, and it's not a pleasant or productive way to treat employees," said the consultant. "Nor does it build people's self-esteem or organizational pride."

"So to build pride in organizations, you need to emphasize what people are doing right," I said.

"And when you do that, the enhanced self-esteem and organizational pride foster sound, ethical decision-making and behavior," said the consultant.

"How do you make sure that your managers actually treat their people well?"

"The best way I know is to have a good, solid performance-review system."

"Why?"

"Because feedback on results is the number-one motivator of people," said the consultant. "We all want to know how well we are doing. When a performance-review system is effective, people are given ongoing feedback on results almost daily, rather than having to wait until a formal performance-review interview. Unfortunately, most organizations either don't have a performance-review system—and therefore people don't really know where they stand—or the established system is simply an organized method of beating people up."

"Our performance-review system falls into that latter category," I said. "Too often managers, including myself, save up negative information about an employee and unload it all at once, either over a minor incident or during his or her performance-review session. Others 'whitewash' the review and act like everything is OK, when it's really not."

"When people are attacked or not dealt with in a truthful manner," said the consultant, "they lose respect for their organization and pride in their jobs."

"That's for sure. Do you know any companies with good performance-review systems?" I asked.

"Unfortunately, such companies are few and far between," said the consultant. "As I travel around the country, I always ask people whether they are pleased with their company's performance-review system, and I can't remember any group ever saying 'yes' except a personnel group that designed the system being used."

"What do you think the problem is with most review systems?"

"I think it's a misdirected emphasis. You see, there are three parts of a good performance review: First, *performance planning*—that's where you set the goals and objectives and the performance standards; second, *day-to-day coaching*—that's where managers roll up their sleeves and help people accomplish their goals; and third, *performance evaluation*—that's where you sit down with your people and evaluate performance against the goals that were set. Now with which one of those three parts of performance review do most organizations start?"

"Performance evaluation," I said. "Personnel comes up with some kind of form that needs to be filled out once or twice a year."

"You've got it," said the consultant. "Most companies start with evaluation and then maybe move to performance planning as management starts to emphasize the importance of goal setting. Which of the three parts of performance review is the one that never seems to be done on a systematic basis?"

"Day-to-day coaching," I said. "I see what you're getting at. All the emphasis is on evaluation with some on performance planning but very little, if any, attention is directed toward coaching or supporting and helping employees win."

"Add to that the 'normal distribution curve' mentality found in most companies, and you've got a very unmotivating system," said the consultant.

"The 'normal distribution curve' mentality?" I echoed.

"In many performance-review systems, when it comes to evaluation, managers are expected to sort out their people according to what you would find if you took a typical sample of the normal population—a few high performers, a few low performers, and then everyone else. The majority would fall in the middle and be considered average performers."

"In other words, only a few people are allowed to win."

"Precisely," continued the consultant. "Suppose you have six or seven people reporting to you and you rate them all high on performance evaluation, how do you think your boss will rate you?"

"He'd consider me a weak manager and rate me down. He'd say I was a 'soft touch' or I was 'giving away the farm' or 'nobody gets a perfect ten.'"

"It's almost as if there is a problem if no one gets rated as poor," agreed the consultant. "So it doesn't take a manager long to realize that the only way he or she can be rated high is to rate some employees low. Now, under that system, the worst thing a manager can have is a group of high performers because then who are you going to rate low? And if you do have a poor performer, you certainly won't want to help him or her because then you wouldn't have anyone to rank as low."

"You're describing our performance review system almost to a T," I interjected. "Now I know why managers are always trying to find fault with the people who work for them."

"Every time you psychologically beat up someone," said the consultant, "you not only tear down that person's self-esteem, but you diminish any respect he or she might have had toward you as a manager or toward the organization. When this practice is widespread throughout the organization, it produces a 'me first' environment, where people act only in their own self-interests."

"How do you take a negative climate and make it positive?" I asked.

"One of the best ways to build self-esteem and pride in organizations is to have a performance-review system with clear goals and measurable performance standards. You also need managers who are willing to roll up their sleeves and support, listen, facilitate, and cheerlead their people to achieve their goals.

"With this kind of performance planning and day-to-day coaching, what do you think happens when performance is evaluated?"

"People win," I said.

'You bet they do," said my friend. "And so does the organization. Life is all about winning and helping others to win."

"Are the goals you set in this process tough ones to achieve?" I queried.

"They can be. People don't mind stretching if they know their manager wants them to win. In a company where praise and encouragement are the rule rather than the exception, employees gain confidence in themselves."

"Do you want people to mentally pat themselves on the back?" I asked.

"Absolutely," replied the consultant. "But remember, that's only possible when people initially feel good about themselves."

"This all sounds great," I said, "but I just can't imagine my boss ever accepting the notion of openly praising and encouraging employees. He thinks of his role as judge and jury combined. One of the insights that came out of my discussion with our mutual advisor friend was the realization that my manager acts the way he does because he doesn't feel very good about himself. How can you ever get bosses who have a low self-esteem to see the world in a positive way?"

"When was the last time you hugged your boss?" asked the consultant.

"You're not serious," I laughed.

"I'm not talking about literally hugging the guy," said the consultant. "I'm asking when was the last time that you *caught your boss doing something right*? Most people, I fear, treat their bosses pretty much the way their bosses treat them. You have to remember that pride and self-esteem are important to managers too. If your boss does something right, what do you usually do?"

"Nothing," I answered truthfully. "I say to myself, 'He gets paid enough. He *ought* to do things right.'"

"Exactly," said the consultant. "And when he does something wrong, what do you do?"

"I usually let him know, directly or otherwise, that he goofed. I see what you're getting at," I reflected. "I accent the negative with my boss, just as he does with me."

"Don't feel bad," the consultant reassured me. "Most people are like you. They never let the boss know when they appreciate his or her efforts. If a manager is like the one you work for and doesn't think much of himself, his feelings of inferiority can be reinforced by the way he is treated. When the boss sees you coming, he'll be ready for a win-lose power struggle because he feels you are always catching him doing things wrong. This makes him feel worse. If you want to make a difference in that relationship, you have to consciously start to reverse the negative feedback you're giving your boss."

"So catching people doing things right should be practiced up, down, sideways—in every direction in the organization," I said.

"Yes," said the consultant. "It's hard to praise others and build up their self-esteem if you don't feel good about yourself."

"What's the impact of all this on customers?" I wondered.

"Customers are directly affected by how people working in the organization are treated," said the consultant. "If the employees don't feel cared for, how can they be expected to care about customers? One top manager I know has over eight hundred employees working for him. When I walked around his operation, I was amazed. He seemed to know every employee's name, what they did, and where they came from. I asked him 'How do you do that—remember everybody's name and background?' He said, 'How can I ask our people to take care of our customers if I won't make any effort to take care of them?' In fact, if you want a good indication of the quality of your people management, ask your customers how they are being treated by your employees. And what is the sweetest sound you can hear coming from someone else's lips?"

"**Y**OUR name," I said. "I think I understand now about the role of true pride in fostering sound, ethical business practices. Everyone who works in the organization has to have pride in what they are doing and when that pride is present, people want to uphold the integrity of their organization. What about patience in organizations? How does that fit in?"

"*Patience* in organizations," explained the consultant, "involves trusting that your values and beliefs are right over the long term. For management, this means focusing on long-term aspects of the business, such as the quality of your product or service and the strength of your relationships with customers, suppliers, and the community in which you conduct business, not just on short-term, bottom-line results. For nonmanagement personnel, patience means being dedicated to doing a good job and knowing that such dedication will ultimately get you to where you want to go in the organization. For all employees, patience means investing energy and adhering to the overall purpose and agreed-upon policies and procedures of the organization. A statement that I love says it well:

*

*Managing **Only**
For Profit
Is
Like
Playing Tennis
With
Your Eye
On The Scoreboard
And Not
On The Ball*

*

"In analyzing any organization," continued the consultant, "it is important to separate the *result* (for example, profits) from the *process* (that is, how you decide to operate and treat people while attempting to achieve your goals and objectives). Sound ethical practices occur in organizations where the previously agreed-upon decision-making process is not compromised or bypassed to achieve desired results."

"In other words, if you don't keep your eye on the ball, you may not get much on the scoreboard."

"That's a good way of putting it," said the consultant. "Everyone agrees that without reasonable results an organization will collapse. At the same time, while results are essential, they alone are not sufficient. If the established process is not followed because of impatience in achieving results, those results may be short-lived. If you take shortcuts to save money at the expense of producing a quality product, or if you show a lack of concern for the long-term interests of your employees or customers, your shortsightedness will cause the organization to fail. Customers will discover that your product lacks quality and will not buy other products your company makes. Employees may start to engage in dysfunctional behavior like lying or stealing, thus trying to undermine the company in an effort to 'get even.' Why? Because customers and employees feel they have been treated poorly.

"In many organizations, there is a shortsighted style of managing, in which employees are mistreated; I call this 'seagull management.'"

"Seagull management," I repeated. "I've heard of a lot of different management styles, but I've never heard about seagull management."

"A seagull manager," smiled the consultant, "flies in, makes a lot of noise, dumps on everyone, and then flies out. That often starts a ripple effect."

After I had a good laugh I said, "A ripple effect?"

"Yes, that's when your boss hears that something has gone wrong—he or she attacks and blames you. In frustration, you beat up on one of your people, who in turn blames someone on an even lower level, or worse yet, takes it out on a customer. In one of his classic *Saturday Evening Post* covers, Norman Rockwell depicted a wonderful example of this ripple effect. The first frame showed a guy being chewed out by his boss, the next frame showed him yelling at his wife, the third frame had his wife screaming at their little boy, and the last frame showed the little boy about to kick his cat."

"The truth of that almost hurts," I said. "And after saying that you're no good and can't be trusted, managers then expect you to be honest, loyal, and all those wonderful things."

"I get calls all the time from companies whose managers want me to look at, among other things, their quality circles. They tell me, 'They're just not functioning the way they're supposed to. We're not getting very good suggestions from our people.'

"In almost every case, I find widespread seagull management, and a 'beat 'em up' performance review system. Exit interviews are often like a James Bond movie. You hear a shout and then somebody has disappeared down a chute. You say, 'Who was that?' The answer: 'I don't know, but keep your mouth shut or you might be next.'

"And then top managers wonder," continued the consultant, "why, when they bring people together and ask for suggestions for improvement, the employees look around the room and try to identify who's the biggest, baddest person in the room who can hurt them the most. Then they say exactly what that person most wants to hear, which in many cases is very different from the truth. Covering up, evading, and passing the buck all become common practices when people have been or anticipate being mistreated."

"And all because the results aren't big enough or coming fast enough," I said. "That's what's happened in our organization—results are getting all the attention."

"A statement like 'I don't care how you get the results—just get them' is a dead giveaway that the short run is being emphasized more than the long run," agreed the consultant.

"Exactly," I said. "Combine seagull management with too little concern for customer service or product quality and you have a disaster waiting to happen."

"Most ethical deterioration you find in an organization can be traced to impatience in attaining goals and objectives. That impatience compromises customer and employee satisfaction and begins a negative cycle that affects results," said the consultant.

"How do you turn around a negative situation similar to the one in my organization?" I wondered.

"Very slowly," said the consultant. "It will probably take two to five years of concentrated effort. It starts with a clear purpose and is maintained with patience. Remember the elderly chairman of Matsushita Electric who thought of himself as the soul of the organization. Someone asked him, 'Does your company have long-range goals?'

"'Yes' was his answer.

"'How long are your long-range goals?'

"'Two hundred and fifty years,' he said.

"'What do you need to carry them out?'

"'Patience.'"

We both had a good laugh. "That's what I call real patience," I said.

"It sure is," said the consultant. "You see, I firmly believe that impatience is the villain that so often drives us off course. What we need in organizations is faith to stick to the values we ultimately believe in and trust that in the long run we will accomplish our objectives. I heard a beautiful example of patience from the president of a high-tech company in New York which makes instruments for doctors. Last spring they turned down a government contract worth over $1 million because they felt the product the government wanted wasn't up to their own company standards even though it would have passed the government standards for acceptable quality."

"**I** ASKED the president if they could have used the business," the consultant continued. "He said, 'You can always use additional business. However, in the long run, delivering an inferior-quality product is not good business. Our family has run this company for the past fifty years and we've learned that if we're patient, better business is around the corner.'"

"So patience is trusting the process and your beliefs and having faith that things will work out," I said.

"That's it," said the consultant. "But one caution about patience. You have to be realistic. Lots of farmers were patient, trusted the process and had faith—yet lost everything. It's hard to trust the process in a steel mill today since the steel industry is in decline. You must believe in yourself, your product, your organization, but you must also be knowledgeable about the real world and prepare yourself for a multitude of scenarios."

"In other words," I said, "don't be naïve. You must be realistic about the future of your organization. I think I understand how patience plays a part in organizations. Tell me about the fourth P—organizational persistence."

"*Persistence* in organizations means that management sticks to its commitment. It does what it said it was going to do. Agreements are kept."

"It seems to me that the managers who turned down that big government contract were not only patient but were also persistent in sticking to their high standards," I said, "It sounds like patience and persistence are closely related."

"Clearly they are," he replied. "If you have faith you will eventually succeed, then you are more apt to persist and behave on your good intentions.

"Of course, some managers break their commitments," he continued. "They issue pious statements about ethical commitment, but do not practice what they preach. For example, they speak eloquently about the values of honesty, integrity, and sincerity—but the company advertising that they have approved consists of misrepresentations, exaggerations, and sometimes outright lies.

"In other organizations, managers who do not persistently uphold established standards of ethical behavior are not held accountable for their lack of commitment. Without accountability—positive or negative consequences of actions or inactions—any policy or program is apt to fail."

"So persistence in organizations involves consistently adhering to the ethical standards and vision that the organization has established," I suggested.

"Precisely," said the consultant. "I recently saw an example of such organizational persistence. Several years ago, before this company had established an Ethics Code and Standards of Behavior policy, it was common practice for many employees to accept gifts from individuals they worked with outside the company. In the new code it was clearly spelled out that employees were not to accept gifts of any kind from customers, suppliers, contractors, and similar individuals when such gifts could influence a current or future business decision. One general manager had made a national search for a key member of his management team to handle corporate contracts. After several months of intensive interviewing, he was very pleased to hire a person with all the necessary qualities and skills.

"The contract manager seemed to be working out very well until one day the general manager happened to be walking by the new manager's office as the phone was ringing. Since the contract manager wasn't there and no one else was answering the phone, the general manager answered it. He said the contract manager wasn't in and asked if the caller wanted to leave a message. The caller responded. 'Just tell him the new contract arrived today and we sent the case of wine as he requested.'

"The general manager knew that a contract had been recently awarded to a new supplier, but this was the first he had heard about any wine. It sounded somewhat suspicious, so he left a note on the contract manager's desk to see him ASAP.

"When the contract manager came by, the general manager gave him the telephone message and asked what it meant. The contract manager said, 'The supplier was simply glad to get the contract and wanted to start the relationship off right. He asked if there was anything he could get me to show his appreciation and I said—half jokingly—"How about a case of wine?" I guess he took me seriously.'

"The general manager deliberated for a moment and then asked, 'Do you know what the company policy on gifts is?'

"'Not to take them.'

"'What are you going to do with this case of wine?'

"'Send it back.'

"'Good,' said the manager, obviously pleased. 'Everyone is entitled to one mistake—you just got yours. You're lucky I caught wind of this early because if I had found out after the fact, you would have been fired.'"

"Would he really have fired the guy?" I asked.

"Yes. He viewed an unenforced policy as worthless to the company. Once word got around that someone had violated the policy and not been punished, there would have been a precedent for others in the company to disregard it as well. In fact, he did have to fire the same manager about six months later over a similar incident. Finding another qualified contract manager was not easy and took several months, but the general manager felt he had to be persistent in consistently applying the policy.

"The manager was not about to compromise on an agreement he had made to live by the Ethics Code and Standards of Behavior established for the company. He stuck to his guns and remained accountable to himself and to his company. He was committed to his commitment."

"So persistence in this case meant not compromising," I affirmed. "How does perspective relate to organizations?"

"*Perspective* in organizations occurs when key members of the organization take time to assess and reflect on where the organization is, where it is going, and how it is going to get there. Too many managers have a 'Ready, Fire, Aim' philosophy. That may promote innovation and experimentation, but it is not appropriate for managing either people or organizations. What you want in managers is a logical 'Ready, Aim, Fire' approach to management."

"What you're talking about is planning," I suggested.

"Yes," said the consultant. "At an organizational level this means taking adequate time for strategic planning and analysis of past and current performance. By doing this the organization is deliberately laying the foundation for future success.

"It also means," continued the consultant, "a choice of how to best make decisions. I've observed a lot of managers who are rapid-fire decision-makers. They spend very little time planning or reflecting. They often short-cut any process that involves other people in decision-making. They don't allow time for weighing the pros and cons of a decision, obtaining additional information, or discussing the decisions with members of their staffs. As a result, often the decision is not balanced."

"That style of managing doesn't foster commitment, does it?"

The consultant nodded in agreement. "Without the commitment of others the implementation of decisions often bogs down or gets sabotaged. The shoot-from-the-hip managers spend a lot of unproductive time cleaning up the mess they've made," he said.

"You're suggesting that it would be better to spend more time planning, reflecting and involving people up front before making any final decision. And if you do that, it will take less time to effectively carry out decisions."

"Absolutely!" said the consultant. "If managers would think and reflect more often before they acted, valuable energy could be used to do things right the first time rather than be wasted on correcting what went wrong. I strongly believe:

*

*If
We
Take Care
In The
Beginning,
The
End
Will
Take Care
Of
Itself*

*

"To take care in the beginning," continued my friend, "you need some way to step back from things and get them in perspective. If you do that, your purpose or mission will become clearer, you are more apt to be patient and persistent in reaching the organizational goals, and pride in the organization will increase."

"Isn't there a danger that you can overplan, think too much, and get caught in paralysis by analysis?" I asked.

"Of course there is. Too much of anything can be a problem. What's required is balance—balance between planning and implementation and between reflection and action."

"What I hear you saying is that we need to make decisions more slowly with adequate reflection," I said.

"Good business requires more thought than simply calculating which choice will make the most money. Remember:

*

*Sometimes
When The
Numbers Look
Right
The Decision
Is Still
Wrong!*

*

"How else can an organization develop perspective?"

"I've seen some interesting approaches to gaining perspective in organizations," said the consultant. "I like one in particular. I know a manager who uses a three-step approach when faced by a serious problem or when an important decision has to be made. The *first* order of business when he calls his team together is *information gathering*. Everyone is asked to contribute and the object is volume—to amass as much information about the problem or decision as possible.

"*Second,* after sharing the information and evaluating ideas with his staff," continued the consultant, "he takes time to *get agreement* on what he calls the *Right Question*. The group works together to arrive at a consensus on the exact wording of a question that, if answered, will yield the best solution possible. For example, 'How can we reduce overhead expenses without laying off people?' He writes out this question in front of the group and asks everyone to study it. Now comes the novel part—the *third* step, which he calls '*inward listening*.' He asks each person to sit quietly for ten minutes and look for the answer to the Right Question from within."

"He doesn't tell them to do anything other than to 'look for the answer within'?" I asked.

"That's right," said the consultant, "and the results are interesting too. He says people do a variety of things in that ten minutes. Some relax and meditate, some reflect calmly on the information that can lead them to an answer, and some even pray, asking for guidance from a higher power. What's fascinated him the most is not what people do, but the results that come out of these quiet sessions. He has been amazed by the creativity and the clarity of thought that emerge. And it also seems to have a harmonious effect on the team—they almost always agree more easily on what should be done, and feel right about their decision. He reports that conflicts seem to disappear. The thinking of the group becomes so much better than the thinking of any single individual that a synergy occurs."

"That really is extraordinary," I said. "We have all kinds of meetings in our company but I think most of them are a waste of time. People interrupt each other, repeat themselves, change the topic, and engage in all kinds of personal power plays and disruptive behavior. We seem to just go around in circles. Whoever came up with the adage 'A camel is a horse designed by a committee' must have had our company in mind."

"I know what you mean," said the consultant. "Getting individuals to think as a team takes time."

"And patience," I added.

The consultant continued, "In addition to taking time with your department to reflect and take stock on an ongoing basis, I recommend an annual or semiannual retreat with your group. Several companies I know have a periodic 'Day of Excellence' where, in addition to some creative or social activity, they set aside some quiet time as a group to reflect on a few key questions, such as, 'What are we feeling good about as an organization (or department)?' 'What should we be doing differently with our business?' And 'To what extent, and how, are we living up to our good intentions?'"

"Let me review for a moment," I said. "Achieving perspective entails making it a priority to set aside time to monitor the organization's well-being. It's like taking the pulse of the organization. It's a matter of avoiding doing things so fast that you don't know whether or not you are doing the right things."

"To me," said the consultant, "perspective in companies or departments involves making sure that what you say is congruent with what you actually do. If you periodically check for such congruence, the organization is more apt to stay on course toward achieving desired goals. In other words, organizational perspective can make a significant and positive difference."

"I think I now understand what you mean when you talk about perspective in organizations. So the Five Principles of Ethical Power really do apply to organizations as well as to each of us individually."

"Yes, they do," said the consultant. "I'm sure our mutual advisor friend gave you a card summarizing the Five Principles of Ethical Power for Individuals. Well, I have prepared a summary of these same principles for organizations."

*The Five Principles of Ethical Power
for Organizations*

1. **Purpose:** The mission of our organization is communicated from the top. Our organization is guided by the values, hopes, and a vision that helps us to determine what is acceptable and unacceptable behavior.

2. **Pride:** We feel proud of ourselves and of our organization. We know that when we feel this way, we can resist temptations to behave unethically.

3. **Patience:** We believe that holding to our ethical values will lead us to success in the long term. This involves maintaining a balance between obtaining results and caring how we achieve these results.

4. **Persistence:** We have a commitment to live by ethical principles. We are committed to our commitment. We make sure our actions are consistent with our purpose.

5. **Perspective:** Our managers and employees take time to pause and reflect, take stock of where we are, evaluate where we are going and determine how we are going to get there.

I FINISHED reading the summary. "That's very helpful. It gives me a powerful and practical strategy for creating a positive environment, one that will foster both ethical decision-making and good performance."

"Let me underline one thing," suggested the consultant. "Many people I talk to about using the Five P's of Ethical Power tell me that it's too bad 'such and such' a person (usually their boss or some top manager) isn't here. He or she could really benefit from this information."

"That's true about my boss and the top managers in our company," I said.

"There is no doubt that it really helps if the top managers—in fact, all the managers—are exposed to the Five P's and become believers," said the consultant. "But Rome was not built in a day. You have to start somewhere and that place could be with your own department. How do you picture your department operating? What are the values, hopes, and dreams you have for personal, group, and company ethical behavior? You have to start with something—a purpose, a vision— before you can become persistent about it."

"Are you advising, Don't take on the whole company right away, particularly if you are a middle manager like me?" I asked.

"That's what I'm getting at," agreed my friend. "If you choose to stay in your present company, you need to realize that the two hardest things for people to remember, once they have learned the Five P's and want to apply them, are patience and pride. People tend to want everything to happen 'yesterday.' At the same time, they get overly caught up in being right. Their pride gets in the way of the very changes they want to bring about."

"You said, if I choose to stay in my company. What do you mean by that?" I asked.

"It seems to me that you have three choices when you find yourself in an environment or organizational culture that is inconsistent with your values and beliefs. The first choice is to resign—leave the organization—and either become an entrepreneur and start your own business or join another company that appears to offer a more compatible ethical culture."

"I've certainly thought about that lately," I said. "But it's not easy to switch jobs and companies—and even more difficult to start one's own business."

"That's why people often select one of the other two choices," said the consultant. "One of those choices is to stay in your present position but mentally isolate yourself from what is going on. However, this outward loyalty and inner doubt can undermine your own spirit. It can be a lonely and excruciating experience."

"It would also make it difficult for me to look at myself in the mirror," I added.

"I agree," said the consultant. "However, many people are able to stay in an incompatible organization by shifting their attention from ethical dilemmas to the problems of managing their department. In other words, you could decide not to worry about the ethical climate and just concentrate on running the most efficient and profitable sales division possible."

"It would be hard for me to isolate myself mentally," I said. "I don't see how I could turn my back on the unethical things going on around me. My work is too important a part of my life. What's the other choice?"

"Stay and try to change the situation," said the consultant. "I figure that's what you'll probably try to do. That's why I emphasized patience and pride in achieving one's vision. Always remember the saying attributed to Father Keller:

*

It
Is
Better
To Light
One Candle
Than
Curse
The
Darkness

*

PATIENCE and pride. True patience and balanced pride. I keep saying those words over and over as I reflect on the last year and a half. It's hard to believe that eighteen months have passed since I first learned about the three Ethics Check questions from my friend and the Five Principles of Ethical Power from the advisor and the consultant. So much has happened since then.

After my meeting with the consultant, I decided to stay with my company and see if I could help change the ethical environment. I swallowed my pride and was patient. I started with my own department and attempted to build a positive work environment. We even defined our department's mission from our customers' perspective and sought to satisfy their needs. I also worked on building a trusting relationship with my boss. While it was difficult to catch him doing something right (I wasn't used to looking), I was successful on occasion and made sure he knew that I had noticed. I realized that once the people I supervised were committed to high performance as well as the power of ethical management, I could then gradually influence other individuals who were higher in the organization.

I had started to see some slow but sustained changes in behavior and attitude as people began to feel good about themselves and the power of ethical management to generate positive results.

Unfortunately, every time I thought I had made some progress, some crisis would come up and seagull management would take over. The emphasis would quickly shift to bottom-line concerns and an ethical environment would be forgotten. I felt like a yo-yo. I didn't think this would ever be a Fortunate 500 company.

I talked it over with my wife several weeks ago and we decided that it would be best if I tried to get another position. I began looking. I got a call from another high-tech company but not in our same industry. They were looking for a new sales manager, a position similar to the one I had. I took a vacation day and visited the company. I was interviewed by all of their top people including the president and the chairman. It was the practice of their top management, they said, to meet and talk with all the likely candidates for key positions. The more I spoke with people in this organization, the more I realized we were on the same wavelength. Their management seemed to have strong ethical values and, from everything I could find out, they practiced what they preached. I was offered the job.

I made up my mind to take the new position. I decided, however, that before I cut my ties with my present company, I would take one last action suggested by my inner voice. I planned a trip to headquarters and made an appointment with the chairman of the board of the company I was leaving.

At our meeting, I put all bitterness and cynicism aside: "Sir," I said, "I don't want to act like a know-it-all or a saint. This company has been good to me and I want to be helpful." Then I told the chairman frankly and honestly why I was planning to leave and why I felt the company's leadership was not fostering ethical behavior among its employees.

The chairman seemed taken aback. He said he wanted to verify the things I had told him. He thanked me for being candid and honest, and for caring enough to talk with him. We parted on a cordial note and as a last word he asked me not to resign yet, but to give him a few days to absorb the information I'd presented. I said I'd have to let the other company know in a week.

The chairman did check out many of the things we discussed. Quite quickly he came to realize that he had lost contact with what was happening in his organization. His focus on ever-increasing shareholder earnings, while important, had blinded him to the internal problems I had described.

At ten o'clock in the evening about four days after our meeting, the chairman called me at home. He said he had talked with the president and other executives and that they were ready to talk seriously with me about creating a new position where I could help direct a program of ethical realignment for the company. "I would like you to stay and help me and others to turn this situation around," he said. He admitted that the task of turning things around would not be easy, but he hoped I would stay and meet the challenge.

That is the way it stands for me now.

I have an offer for a new position in a company that seems compatible with my beliefs about ethical management. I also have an opportunity to remain at my present company in an official capacity to help bring about needed change. The first choice might be the better one because I'd be more in tune with the environment. That could make me more productive and provide me with a greater sense of fulfillment. However, the second choice might be even more rewarding if I were successful. It certainly would be challenging.

As a result, I now need to make a difficult choice between an exciting opportunity in a new organization or a tough challenge in an old environment . . .

*

*Which
Would
You
Choose?*

*

Acknowledgments

Sir Isaac Newton said it well one time: "If I have seen further it is by standing upon the shoulders of giants."

First, our thanks to *Larry Hughes,* president of the Hearst Trade Book Group, for his vision that brought us together and his support that made this book possible.

Second, we would like to thank the hundreds of managers around the country who read the various drafts of this book and gave us thoughtful feedback and suggestions for improving it. Particular thanks to *Bill* and *Lew Allyn* of Welch Allyn in Skaneateles, New York, and *Robert Small* of the Worthington Hotel in Fort Worth for their example and inspiration.

We would like also to acknowledge the following people:

Jan Abbott for sharing her parable of "The Lost Soul."

Jim Ballard for his creative suggestions and for teaching us about entering our day more slowly.

John Barrons, Dick Neal, Al Pope, Ray Reynanti, and others involved in the Ethics Programs at General Dynamics in San Diego.

Warren Bennis for his contribution on the personal moral dilemmas that you face in staying or leaving an organization that is incongruent with your value system.

Lee Berglund for pointing out that we have all the time there is—it's what we do with that time that counts.

Theodore Brophy, Sol Linowitz, William Mitchell, John Naisbitt, and *Bonita Granville Wrather* for their participation and sharing of ideas at the White House Conference on Ethics, co-sponsored by Cornell University in April 1986.

Howard Cady, retired editor at William Morrow and Company, for his friendship and professional support for Norman Vincent Peale.

Wendy Reid Crisp, Herman Gadon, Natasha Josefowitz, Harvey Mackay, Michael O'Connor, and *Pat Zigarmi* for their thoughtful reading and detailed suggestions for improvement.

Pat Golbitz, our editor, and *Margaret McBride,* our literary agent, for their support throughout the publishing process.

Sybil Light, secretary to Norman Vincent Peale, for her helpfulness throughout this project.

Paul Hersey and *Marshall Goldsmith* for some of their thinking about performance review.

Phil Hodges for his thoughts on pride, patience, and prayer and his continual encouragement.

Morris Massey for emphasizing the importance of going to a viewing place for perspective.

John Naisbitt for the "Fortunate 500" idea.

Bob Nelson for his very able writing assistance throughout this project.

Red Scott for his thoughts on the importance of reflecting about where you are going.

Eleanor Terndrup, secretary to Ken Blanchard, for giving this book her usual tender love, care, and typing excellence.

Art Turock for teaching us the difference between commitment and interest.

About the Authors

Kenneth Blanchard: Few individuals have had as much impact on the day-to-day management of companies as has Kenneth Blanchard, co-author of *The One Minute Manager* and The One Minute Manager Library.

Blanchard, a popular keynote speaker for national conventions, seminars, and business meetings, is a well-known writer, consultant, and teacher. He received his B.A. and Ph.D. from Cornell University. His text *Management of Organizational Behavior: Utilizing Human Resources,* now in its fourth edition, co-authored with Paul Hersey, is considered standard reading on the subject of management.

Dr. Blanchard, with his wife, Margie, is the founder of a management consulting firm, Blanchard Training and Development, Inc., in Escondido, California. He maintains a faculty position in leadership at the University of Massachusetts, Amherst, as well as being on the board of trustees of Cornell University.

Norman Vincent Peale: Dr. Peale is the author of thirty-four books. *The Power of Positive Thinking* is one of the most successful books ever published and has been translated into forty languages, with sales of over 20 million copies worldwide. Dr. Peale's positive thinking philosophy has become an integral part of many cultures.

Dr. and Mrs. Peale are co-editors and publishers of the inspirational monthly magazine *Guideposts*. It has a circulation of 4.6 million paid subscribers, with 16 million readers each month.

Messages by Dr. Peale are released to over a million persons monthly by the Foundation for Christian Living, Pawling, New York. Thirty-five million copies of his inspirational booklets are distributed yearly.

Dr. Peale is a speaker at national business, trade, and sales conventions throughout the United States, Canada, and abroad. He is the recipient of twenty-one honorary doctoral degrees.

Services Available

Drs. Kenneth Blanchard and Norman Vincent Peale speak to conventions and organizations all over the world. They also have their messages available on audio and video tape.

In addition, Blanchard Training and Development, Inc., conducts seminars and in-depth consulting in business ethics, management, and leadership skills.

For further information on Dr. Blanchard's and Dr. Peale's activities and programs contact:

Blanchard Training and Development, Inc.
125 State Place
Escondido, California 92025
619/489-5005

Foundation for Christian Living
P. O. Box FCL
Pawling, New York 12564
914/855-5000

People
With
Humility
Don't
Think
Less
Of
Themselves...

They
Just
Think
About
Themselves
Less

A Selected List of Cedar Books
DIRECT ORDER FORM

Peter Grose Ltd, PO Box 18, Mayhill, Monmouth, Gwent NP5 4YD.

Please send cheque (made out to Peter Grose Ltd) or postal order, or credit card details below, for purchase price quoted and allow the following for postage and packing:

UK, BFPO & Eire £1 for the first book, 50p for each subsequent book ordered, to a maximum charge of £2.00.

Overseas Customers £2.00 for the first book plus 75p for each subsequent book.

NAME (Block Letters) ....

ADDRESS ....

.... Date...

VISA/ACCESS/MASTERCARD/AMERICAN EXPRESS Card No. ....

Expiry date ....

Signature ....

While every effort is made to keep prices low, it is sometimes necessary to increase prices at short notice. Cedar Books reserves the right to show new prices on covers which may differ from those previously advertised.